How I Made My Husband Gay

Myths About Straight Wives

Bonnie Kaye, M.Ed.

CCB Publishing
British Columbia, Canada

How I Made My Husband Gay: Myths about straight wives

Library and Archives Canada Cataloguing in Publication
Kaye, Bonnie, 1951-
How I Made My Husband Gay: Myths about straight wives / by Bonnie
Kaye.
Also available in electronic format.
ISBN 978-0-9784388-4-5
1. Bisexuality in marriage. 2. Closeted gays--Family relationships.
3. Gay men--Family relationships. 4. Gay men--Relations with
heterosexual women. 5. Marital conflict. 6. Self-help techniques.
I. Title.

HQ1035.K39 2007   306.872   C2007-906415-9

Publisher: CCB Publishing
              British Columbia, Canada
              www.ccbpublishing.com

This book is dedicated to the millions of women who have lived with the self-doubt while living with a gay husband.

It is also dedicated to:

- My family members who give me unconditional support
- My soul mate of 14 years who loves me just the way I am and inspires me to continue this mission to help others find our happiness
- The generous women from my support network who were brave and caring enough to share these personal stories to help save others from unnecessary suffering
- The extraordinary women who join me weekly in my support chat
- And to the wonderful gay men in my support network, especially Dennis, Doug, Derrick, and Michael, who generously give their time to support this cause of honesty and sanity

Other books by Bonnie Kaye

Is He Straight: A Checklist for Women Who Wonder

Doomed Grooms: Gay Husbands of Straight Wives

Man Readers: A Woman's Guide to Dysfunctional Men

Straight Wives: Shattered Lives

Preface

You may think the title of this book is shocking, but I wanted to make people think about the absurdity of the possibility. The sad part is that too many people still believe that this is true— we, as straight wives, have some kind of magical power to turn our straight husbands into gay husbands. Even in this day and age, people still DON'T GET IT. For the millions of women who marry gay men, it is quite confusing to understand how this happens... how much more confusing is it for people who just hear about it?

In September of 2006, a dozen of my support group members were traveling from Philadelphia to New York to join with others during my annual New York get-together to launch our first collaborative book, *Straight Wives: Shattered Lives*. At the rest stop before the George Washington Bridge where we freshened up, a gentleman walked over to our group of chatty women sitting in a passenger van. He started talking to us in a friendly way, curious about how we all knew each other. He began guessing if we belonged to the same church, women's organization, or if we were friends traveling to see a Broadway show. We kept shaking our heads "No" after each question. He was truly puzzled. Finally, one woman replied, "We all have gay husbands!" The man started to chuckle. His next question was, "Were they gay when you married them?" He wasn't chuckling then. This was not a new or original question for any of us. It's a question that keeps women in the closet long after their husbands come out.

With all the knowledge and publicity on this topic, too many people believe that homosexuality is a conscientious "choice" that men make. And it is not unusual for people to look at us and wonder where **we,** their wives, failed in the marriage for our husbands to "choose" that road. For this reason, we decided on that day that the next collaborative book would be titled *How I Made My Husband Gay.* Of course, the subtitle is "Myths About Straight Wives." Every woman reading this book hopefully knows that this is a MYTH. But if you still have any doubts or believe in some irrational way that you have anything to do with influencing your husband's homosexuality, hopefully these stories will put your mind to rest.

Contents

*35 stories from straight wives with in depth
details to help other women including:*

- *Red Flags*
- *Blame was the Name of His Game*
- *Sex Tells It All*
- *How I Caught Him*
- *The Truth Behind His Lies*
- *Happily Ever After – For Real*

Introduction

This is my fourth book about Straight Wives and Gay Husbands. Is there anything left to say that hasn't been said already? First, in 2000, there was _Is He Straight? A Checklist for Women Who Wonder_. This book gave women who wondered about their husbands' sexuality a checklist of what to look for if their husbands were gay. Three years later, I wrote _Doomed Grooms: Gay Husbands of Straight Wives_ which was a follow up after you realized your husband's homosexuality to help women understand why this happens. In 2006, I published _Straight Wives: Shattered Lives_, a compilation of stories from 27 of my support group women from around the world who described the pain in their marriages to help other women in this situation make an emotional connection. This book was highly praised by everyone who read it. So many women who were struggling in their marriages recognized themselves in these stories.

So now what? Is there anything that hasn't been said in one form or another? Well, YES! The problem is that over 50% of gay husbands are still closeted in denial about their homosexuality. Therefore, there will always be more to be learned by their wives who live in the darkness of their lies in hopes that they can see the light and realize the truth.

As a counselor for over 30,000 women with gay husbands since 1984, no one has seen more wasted years of unhappiness and struggle in this field than me. The average length of marriage for the women I work with is 22 years. If that is the average, think of how many marriages are even longer. When I think of the pain, confusion, and suffering of so many women who blame themselves for the failure in their marriages which they have no clue about or control over, it makes me very sad. It also makes me very angry. It makes me angry because I believe that life is a gift. No man has the right to take away one moment of our lives from us; imagine taking 10, 20, 30, or 40 plus years away from caring, loving women.

I am the first to say that homosexuality is not an easy admission to make when you grow up in a society that is not accepting and unforgiving. I truly admire those gay people who toss their fate to the wind and don't care. They are open and honest, taking whatever consequences come their way. I even admire gay men who are not open about their homosexuality, but they can accept who they are and don't feel the need to escape from it by marrying a woman.

To go one step further, I am also understanding of those men who marry HOPING against hope that marriage will make them straight when they know they have attractions to men. Most gay men who get married love their wives to the best of their ability. They are not marrying them because they "hate" women or because they are trying to "trick" us. They are actually trying to "trick" themselves into thinking that we will be able to eliminate those feelings they so desperately don't want to feel.

Sometimes marriage works for a while. Some gay men really believe that loving their wives has taken away those nagging male sexual attractions. Love is a powerful thing--at least it is at first. But it is only a matter of time until those attractions start creeping back again, and the desire to act on them becomes so consuming that they become the primary thought on the man's mind. At that point, some men are honest about it and tell their wives. I tell my women that as hard as it is to learn the truth, it is much harder not knowing and wondering why the marriage is failing.

When gay husbands refuse to be honest, it shows that they care more about themselves than their wives. I have heard the excuses including, "I don't want to hurt my wife because I love her," but this is an excuse for men who lack the courage to do the right thing. Love means telling your wife that she is not desirable to you because you are a gay man. Love is telling your wife that her normal sexual urges are being denied because you are a gay man, not because she is a nymphomaniac. Love is letting your wife know that she had nothing to do with these feelings you have for men. You were born this way—she didn't turn you this way.

I wanted to put together a "self-help" book for women who are still confused. Many of my own support group members were clueless for so long. They didn't understand that a gay man could marry them. They thought that gay meant "same sex attraction." If there were problems in the marriage, they came to believe that THEY were the cause of the problems— never guessing what the real problem was.

I asked my group to participate in this book by addressing the following issues that seem to evade our women the most:

1. Red Flags: What signs you missed when you look back?

People feel that we should have known—were we blinded by love? Were we naïve? Didn't we suspect anything was wrong from the beginning? After the marriage, we often say that hindsight is 20/20. There were signs, we just did not see them, believe them, or understand them. I want other women to be able to identify with these signs.

2. Blame was the Name of His Game: How did your husbands blame you for the failures in your marriage rather than take responsibility?

Many of us were blamed for everything that went wrong in our marriages. We were never smart enough, supportive enough, clean enough, or attractive enough. We were too pushy, too domineering, too demanding, or wanted too much sex. Some have actually accused us of "making them gay" for those reasons.

3. Sex Tells It All: The excuses your husbands used to not have sex.

Sex—rather lack of it--is one of the primary problems that most of us faced. Some of our husbands used some incredible excuses not to have sex including medications, illnesses, depression, and work. It seems with their gay male lovers, they do not need to use an excuse.

4. How I Caught Him: How you were able to catch your husbands if you did catch them, helping to give tips to other women.
Some of you were successful by catching them via the Internet, tracking systems, tracing cell phone calls, or other methods. In other words, the detective work you did and how it worked out. You can also mention how you used this information to confront your husband and if he denied it, what excuses he used.

5. The Truth Behind His Lies: What you learned about your husband's activities after his denials.
Most women want to believe that their husbands never acted on their homosexuality during the marriage, only to find out that they were lying from the very beginning and acting on it. This part is extremely important because women need to face the reality that they can be infected with STD's or HIV/AIDS. If they continue to believe their husbands' denials of ever acting on their homosexuality, they build a false sense of security.

6. Happily Ever After – For Real: How you have moved on in your life.
Many women stay stuck in their marriages because they are so beaten down through the years that they believe they can never move on and be happy. If you have restarted your life with a new relationship that has been successful, please share that so other women will realize that there is life again after the death of a marriage to a gay husband. Some of you have found some wonderful relationships/marriages in the aftermath, and I'd like to let women know this is possible.

These were the guidelines. I told the participants that they could write about one of the topics or all of the topics.

At first, I was going to break the book into six chapters and distribute their stories into each category. But then I changed my mind because I wanted my readers to get a sense of who these women are. So I have left the writings in their original format. It is my hope that as you read these stories, you find a connection with your own life if you are still questioning your husband's sexuality. And if you already know the truth, I am hoping that you find a connection with other women so you'll know that you're not alone and not to blame for not recognizing the signs that now may seem so obvious.

Remember, the men who live these lives of deceit are masters of deception. They live a lie every day of their life, and they work very hard on fooling you!

How I Made My Husband Gay:
The Stories of My Women

PROFILE #1: EMMA B., 44, Wisconsin, married 9 years, in process of divorce, one son five years old. I'm an Accountant by trade but became a stay-at-home Mom when my son was born.

I had no idea my husband was gay. He was definitely the pursuer when we first met. He was so head over heels in love with me. I actually broke up with him once when we were dating because I was dating someone else when we met. I was married the first time for five years. My first husband left me for another woman. We had no children. I was 33 when I went through my first divorce. I met my second husband--the gay one-- through a friend while I was still happily married to my first husband. She told him I was not available as I was married. He was very disappointed. However, when my first marriage broke up, the friend told him I became available and we dated for two years before marrying.

My co-workers who knew him while he was courting me thought he was a diamond in the rough. They are were envious of me because of how he courted me, sending me flowers at work on all the special occasions and always buying me the nicest jewelry on birthdays and Christmas.

I was 36 when I married the second time. We tried to have a family right away. After a lot of fertility workup and treatments, I finally got pregnant at 39. My son was a miracle baby. He was born prematurely, weighing less than three pounds. We are very fortunate that he (now five) is a healthy, bright, and an amazing special little boy.

I always thought my husband and I had a good sexual relationship. The frequency wasn't as much as what my first husband wanted. I just thought maybe he had a low sex drive. I made sure we had sex around my fertile time as we were trying to conceive. I always felt that I was the one that initiated the sex; he didn't do much of the initiating. He was a horrible kisser. I hated the way he kissed, but he knew how to please and satisfy me. He was a very giving partner when we had sex. I've often asked him why we couldn't kiss more. He would say because it would lead to sex. I guess that should have been a red flag. I didn't think so because there was nothing gay about him at the time. He was a good husband, always went along with whatever I wanted, and gave me nice jewelry for presents. He always came straight home after work; I always knew where he was. He was attracted to women and has crushes on several female movie stars.

From the very beginning of our marriage, we definitely had communication problems. He grew up in his household where his mother and father would not talk to each other for months at a time. They finally divorced after almost 50 years when they were 69 years old. From early on in our marriage, my husband definitely avoided conflicts and did not communicate well. I had kept a journal and looking back in it now, our marriage was definitely headed for trouble due to his inability to communicate. Again, I never saw any gay tendencies from early on.

My husband was a neat person, very particular about his clothes (he always ironed his own clothes and polished his shoes), and hated clutter. I had always thought that this was due to his Army career for 20 years which was why he was very good at taking care of his own clothes, ironing them, and keeping his shoes polished. I don't know if I should have seen that as being a gay tendency.

The other things about him that might have been different, but nonetheless didn't think they were gay tendencies were the fact he always liked to bake cut-out cookies and decorate them at Christmas time. He also was a better cleaner than I was. He believed in spring-cleaning, taking everything out of our closets and cupboards to do spring-cleaning. He was the youngest of five children: three older sisters and one older brother. His siblings are much older than he is, so he was practically raised by his one sister. He is also very close to his Mom. He grew up baking Christmas cookies with them and helping them do spring cleaning so again I didn't take that as signs of a gay tendency either.

The Start of Our Marital Problems

I think we would both agree that we had a pretty decent marriage for the first five years of our marriage. He would never end a phone call without saying "I love you!" He was very attentive and supportive during my pregnancy with our miracle baby. He even read baby books and magazines in preparation for our son's arrival. Because of my advanced age when my son was born, I knew I wanted to try for our second child shortly after.

During the first year when our son was born, he was a great dad and continued to be a loving husband. When our son was about 18 months old, I remembered that was the first time I had a gut feeling that he was unhappy. He told me if it weren't for our son, he would "walk." I was very surprised he felt that way. Because our son was born so little and we didn't have families near by, we did not really use a baby sitter. We didn't get out much as a couple, though I didn't have any problems with that. I so truly loved being a Mom and wasn't missing out on "going out" at all. We did go to marriage counseling and most of our issues had to do with my husband not communicating and avoiding conflicts.

Still, we continued to attempt to conceive again. We proceeded with IVF to try to get pregnant but due to lack of eggs, the IVF cycle was abandoned. Nonetheless, we continued to try "naturally" on our own to get pregnant. Again, it felt like I was always the one initiating sex during my fertile time but he never complained about it.

Red Flags

About two years ago, my husband started to work out at the Y near his work. He also joined some exercise classes that was taught by a gay instructor, Adam. For two years, rain or snow, he would get up at 5:15am every day to go work out before work. He was very proud of his progress. He kept a log of his exercise routine. After a whole year of working out with this instructor, my husband bought him these special "breathable" exercise socks as a Christmas gift. Also about this time, my husband became quite close to a gay co-worker, Rob, at work. I had met Rob and his live-in partner a few years back and thought nothing of it. They've been to our house for dinner and vice versa. My husband's workplace is very liberal and they have a large population of open gay relationships. During the last two years, they went out to lunch together quite frequently (at least once or twice a week) and always sent each other instant messages. In this last year, my husband told one of my good friends that Rob had become his Best Friend! I was surprised to hear that. Maybe I was just oblivious but I didn't realize their relationship has gotten so close.

In April of last year, while I took our son to visit some friends for two days, Rob took my husband shopping the first night we were gone. He bought a whole new outfit that consisted of a shirt, jeans, shoes, belt and even a new pair of sunglasses. They were clothes of styles that my husband never had before. Looking back that was one of the first signs that something was changing…

Last summer, there were several more scenarios that should have raised some red flags but I wrote them off. One time he took his gay exercise instructor Adam to an INXX concert and they ended up at a gay bar after the concert. My husband had bought the tickets from one his female co-workers, who is heterosexual and married. She and her husband were meeting a gay friend at the gay bar after the concert, so my husband told me that was how he ended up there. He came home telling me about his night out. He seemed excited and sounded like he had fun. He said it was "funny" watching people at the bar. However, he never said he was grossed out or uncomfortable being at the gay bar.

On another occasion, my husband took Rob, his supposedly newfound "Best Friend" to a Josh Turner concert. He actually asked my friend to get him two tickets, telling her they were for him and me to go. He later just told me since I don't know any of his songs anyway, he would take Rob instead since he helped us moved into our new house and it was a way to say "thank you." Call me stupid, but I trusted him, and I didn't think much of that either.

He did buy birthday and Christmas presents for Rob. I was even the one that wrapped them. I honestly thought they were just good friends. In September, he took Rob out for his birthday and I said I hope you don't take him out on his actual birth date as that should be reserved for his partner or Dave would be mad at you...

Shortly before Christmas, my husband and the gay instructor, Adam went to the hospital to visit another gay instructor that was admitted to the hospital for an anal abscess. That night, he didn't get home until almost 11pm. That was the first time he has stayed out late other than when he went to the concerts. He said they went shopping and grabbed a bite to eat afterwards. My husband came home with four bags of clothes from the GAP and Banana Republic, stores where he does not usually shop. He said Adam helped him pick the clothes out because he said my husband wore his clothes way too big--one size larger than he should.

Looking back now, I must have been just so naïve because still at that time, I didn't speculate that there was something going on... although the signs were there. My husband would giggle and acted like a kid whenever he talked about Adam or Rob.

Two weeks before Christmas, my husband loaned Adam, his gay instructor, his SUV to drive 1,000 miles to pick up something he had bought on EBay. I was a little annoyed and upset that he didn't consult with me first, but rather he just told me that he was lending his car out. On the night that my husband was meeting his gay instructor to give him the car for his road trip, he packed him a "care package" with a bottle of water, some fruits, and some homemade Christmas cookies we had just made with our son. Looking back, I guess no straight man would think of putting together a little "care package" for his gay friend!

We spent seven days for Christmas on the East Coast. My husband seemed pretty irritable. In the meantime, I was researching for a cruise for our annual February mid-winter vacation at my husband's request. He wanted to get away and was mad that it was taking me so long to "book" our vacation.

On New Year's Day, after just getting back from our Christmas holiday with my family, my husband was measuring to expand our son's and our master closet after having just moved into our new house in November. He was planning on going to Home Depot that day to get the supplies needed for that project. As usual, my husband's enthusiasm wore off and he never did go to Home Depot or start on that project.

How I Found Out

The day after New Year's when he went back to work after having been away for a week, he found out his best friend Rob was let go from his job. My husband was very upset. He told me he was more upset than Rob was about it. They gave him two weeks notice. His last day would be Friday, January 12.

My husband was even quieter than usual coming home after work during those two weeks leading up to January 12. He said it was just a really busy week at work. During this time, I was emailing him at work with various options for our cruise vacation. He told me he had a big project coming up and now not sure if he could get away in February as he has originally wanted.

On Friday night, January 12, (incidentally it was also my husband's "best friend" Rob's last day at work), while I was putting our son to bed, my husband called out and asked if he could go to the mall. I assumed he was going to make an exchange for something. I said fine as I couldn't ask him more questions since I was reading a bedtime story to our son. After coming out of our son's bedroom and smelling my husband's cologne in our bedroom, I found it strange that he would put cologne on just to go to the mall. I was also getting ready and preparing food for my husband's Mom's and our son's joint birthday celebration the next day. I thought it was odd that he chose that night to go to the mall (something he rarely does) when he should be helping me prepare for the party the next day.

I decided to call him on his cell phone and asked why he was out when we had a party to get ready for and when he was going to be home. He told me he didn't know what time he would be home. Then I pressed, "What is going on?" That's when he dropped the bomb and said "I am filing for divorce next week!" I was shocked!!! What? I had no idea and did not see it coming at all! He said we could talk about it when he got home and hung up. Two hours passed by and I called him again inquiring when he was coming home so we could talk. He said he didn't know. Two additional hours went by, and this time he wasn't answering his cell phone.

Needless to say, I sat in disbelief just waiting for him to come home, anticipating an explanation. He finally walked in at midnight. When I inquired where he was, he said it was no longer any of my concern and that <u>there was nothing to talk about</u>. He said he had taken his wedding ring off for two weeks, and I never even noticed. I asked him if there was someone else and he said "NO!" Right at that moment when I looked into his eyes, that's when I KNEW there was someone else, AND THAT IT WAS ANOTHER MAN!

He slept on the couch that night. I didn't sleep at all that night. Finally at

5 a.m., I knew my son would be getting up soon, so I went to the living room and asked him, "Are you GAY or Bisexual? How could this have happened? We have a child together!" All these questions I had, but he would not say a word or answer me. All he said was "I've been lying to you. I've been pretending. I only acted like I was having a good time when we just had a dinner party the week before." He also told me he went to see a therapist three times that week, and that he couldn't eat and was throwing up. I do believe that was the week he admitted to himself that he is in fact gay.

The next day, he packed a duffle bag of clothes and left. Each time he came back to see our son, he would take carloads of his clothes, and now he has pretty much taken all his clothes and personal belonging. Two weeks later, on the weekend of our son's fifth birthday, he served me with divorce papers.

Denial

That "Bomb Drop" was about five months ago. To this day, he still has not come out to admit that he is gay. I have repeatedly begged him to please be honest with me for the sake of us being able to work together to co-parent our son. He won't. He is a coward, a man with absolutely no integrity, and I have lost all respect of him for how he has handled this situation.

The Truth

At first, I thought his relationship was with Rob, but during these past five months, I found out he has been living with Adam, his gay instructor. He took Adam to San Francisco during Spring Break Week. Adam was still in school at the time studying to be a nurse but just graduated this month. My husband has become quite the Sugar Daddy. He is 42 years old, and his boyfriend just turned 30. My husband makes a very good salary, and we have had a very good standard of living. Since he left us, he spends all his money on Adam and won't even provide my son and me money for food and necessities. Our divorce pre-trial is coming up in two weeks.

My husband has bought a whole new wardrobe since he left, with styles of clothing that he never wore in the 12 years that I knew him. He has lost about 25 pounds and dropped down two sizes from his normal Large or XL to now a Small in size. He also has a new hairstyle. He used to wear his hair super short and cut it every 6 weeks, but now he leaves it curly and longer at the top. He has trimmed down in size and wears clothes that look very homosexual to me, not feminine but just boyish like.

The Blame Game

I have to say one of the worst parts of dealing with my husband being gay is the blame thing. He honestly believes that I am the blame for everything! It saddens me that he twists things to make me out to be a horrible person, and that I was a bad wife that didn't work with him or loved him. He tells me **I am** the reason why he had to divorce me, and that I had control issues.

I begged him to be honest with me, to come clean and explain to me what happened to him so that I can have closure and to be able to better deal with him and to co-parent with him for our son in the future. He won't. Instead, he talks to me belligerently, full of anger, blames me for everything and treats me with such hostility.

I walked on eggshells around him for many years with the silent treatment, and he always snapped at me. I couldn't make him happy no matter what I did. He would complain how long it took me to do grocery shopping. I would race home when I thought I'd been gone longer than one hour, speeding through red lights just to get home so he wouldn't be angry with me. He complained I talked too long on the phone with my best friends from my home state, even though I would do it after he and my son went to bed so it wasn't during our family time. I stopped talking to my friends all together. I lived like a prisoner in my own home. Even though I was a successful professional woman when I worked before my son was born, I lost all of my self-esteem from all his years of criticizing me. He became a non-loving and non-supportive husband. His betrayal is horrendous and unimaginable.

He said to me "You have been so controlling of me, and so unsupportive of me as a husband that I really don't know why I did not do this earlier. He said I was manipulative and that I drove him away! He told me he finally made the choice of being happy and not continue to fake a loving relationship that was so one-sided. He is even claiming that the love was his side! He said I was not a partner in our marriage. "If I had really felt that we were a mutually contributing couple then maybe I would still be with you today."

This is an excerpt form an email he sent me after he filed for divorce. "The counselors said you were controlling and that if you did not change you will lose your husband. Guess what - you lost me. You ask what I have become. Really it's a happy person. I feel so bad about having to leave our son but I am so sure that this is the right thing. Granted there are two sides to this but if you could have been a better "partner" this would not have had to happen. "

He went as far to say, **"If I am gay, bi or whatever, it has nothing to do with me filing for divorce no matter what you may think."**

Self-discovery

Through therapy, I learned that even if I did everything the way he wanted, he still wouldn't have been happy with me because he is gay. I learned that I didn't make him gay and I didn't drive him away to be a homosexual. I am still struggling with how he could be so angry with me. I do honestly believe that he didn't know he was gay when he met me, fell in love, and married me. I believe he realized how comfortable and happy he was once he met Adam in the past two years and came to realize that's who he is and who he would rather be with. I always thought he was a great dad and he does love his son, but his need to be with another man far outweighs his love for his only child.

PROFILE #2: DOLLIE W., 54, Washington, married 28 years, separated, two children, Annie, age 22 and Marc, age 16. I'm from a Catholic religious background, and was from a good family. I went to an all-girls Catholic high school and didn't date at all in high school. I dated very little in college. I went to a 'commuter' college, so I didn't make a lot of friends at school. In my early 20's I dated more, but still didn't have a long-term relationship until I met my gay husband.

Red Flags

The first red flag that I should have picked up on was when we were dating. I'd want to hold his hand, but his palms sweated so badly, we both gave up on that. I just thought it was a peculiarity of his. But he was always distant. Even his friends from work commented to him that he's a hard one to get to know. When he proposed, he never said the words, "Will you marry me?" He said, "I care for you deeply," showed me the ring, and asked me what I thought about it. I couldn't believe it when I saw Dina McGreevy's interview on Oprah! She said her husband said the same thing to her when he "proposed" to her! My husband told me that he talked with friends of his in the Air Force, and he told them that he wasn't sure if I'd accept. They asked him why. He said, "I don't know." Looking back, it was probably because of the "love" thing. He couldn't bring himself to tell me that he LOVED me, and he was wondering himself if "I care for you deeply" would cut it. I just thought he was shy.

So we got married. At first everything was fine. Then he started getting in little digs at me. First, he called me stupid when I went to the store and didn't get the right thing that he asked for. Next, he told me how *beautiful* his sister looked on her wedding day. I told him that he never commented on how I looked on _our_ wedding day, even though I told him how great he looked. Then he said, "You looked _nice_." Then there was, "There isn't anything I wouldn't do for my sister." Their typical manner is throwing you off-guard every chance they get – making you "second-guess" everything they say. So I'm thinking, "Well, he married me, so I am assuming that he would feel the same way about me."

Six years went by, and I was pregnant with our daughter. I told him then and before that I loved him, to which he replied, "uh huh." After our daughter was born, he was absolutely NO HELP! I had post-partum depression and an undiagnosed thyroid problem. I was exhausted because of both AND was up at night with the baby. He never once got out of bed to help unless the baby was sick **and** throwing up in her crib.

I felt like he gave the orders, and I had to obey him, as if I were a child. My opinion didn't matter to him at all--ever. I realized he was narcissistic, and he made me very unhappy. He never joked; everything was serious with him. He had frequent 'hissy-fits" and temper tantrums. His behavior got worse with time.

On day when I was pregnant with my second child 17 years ago, I was cleaning the closet and found condoms in his jacket pocket. I confronted him and he told me that he had been to some xxx rated movies and jacked himself off, using the condoms to catch the mess. Gay didn't even enter my mind. Yes, admittedly I was naïve, but I thought our marriage was based on truth, so I believed him. I do remember one thing he said at the time, and for some reason, it stuck in my head, after all these years. During our conversation, he said, "It just feels so natural." I thought then, "Hmm – what feels so natural – masturbating?" It just seemed odd.

All the while, I kept thinking that if I tried harder, he would "get better," until he moved our family on a farm three years ago. He used the farm as a tax shelter and used me to be his farm hand while he was away during the week, coming home on weekends. He needed a tax shelter because he was going through so much cash, and he had expensive charges on credit cards. Just before he asked for a divorce was when his behavior got really weird!

Blame was the Name of His Game

Larry's behavior began getting 'twilight-zone'-like, when we were on our family vacation in June, 2006, in Hawaii. He dumped our daughter, son, and me off at one beach while he went to a nude beach. He came back to pick us up four hours later, when it was dark. He hiked to the nude beach on another day while the children and I were at the beach next to the nude beach. I stayed to watch our children while they swam in the ocean, and while Larry walked to the nude beach. He got up in the middle of the night and used his computer. He went on other solo excursions while leaving us alone in the condo. He went on some excursions with us, but never got in the water. He was disconnected. It appeared like he was looking right through me, never walking with me, always well ahead. He didn't fly over there with us, and he departed a day after us. He said he couldn't get the same reservations as my son and me because he wanted to use his frequent-flyer miles. I noticed after we got back home that he had a tattoo on his ankle.

He had lost weight, grown a beard, and spruced up his wardrobe. He told me that a female captain at work told him that she liked his beard, and he should never shave it off. Okay, there's another woman, I thought.

In early October 2006, Larry said he wanted a divorce. He told me, "I don't love you and I never have. I don't have empathy, and I don't know where to get it. We were never meant to be together. We've grown apart." I made it quite clear that I didn't like "his" farm, while he left me during the week, expecting me to water 400 blueberry bushes. Then he would come home on most weekends, only to work out in the field, and then leave again for another week or more. So he made ME feel like "we've grown" apart, because "I" didn't like his farm. He also added, "You should find someone else now." He told me multiple times, "There's no one else." He also told me about a guy at work whose wife had a stroke recently, and now that guy has to take care of his wife! He was concerned that something similar could happen to us. I simply could not believe what I was hearing!

Prior to this, I asked him to please go to counseling. He said he went to counseling and talked about getting a divorce. I even asked him if he was gay at the request of a few friends of mine who suspected it. He answered, "No," even with a chuckle!

All those hurtful words didn't make sense at the time. How could this person I married be so cold? It was like he wanted to hurt me on purpose. It wasn't until the VISA bill came that I saw that he had charged $3,500 for an attorney. Until I opened the bill, I thought from what he told me, that he was going to *mental health counseling.* Larry couldn't even tell me that he had retained an attorney. I had to find that out when I opened the credit card bill.

I began to go for counseling. I tried one counselor then switched to a different counselor. Both counselors told me that Larry would fall under the heading of Narcissist Personality Disorder, which is a recognizable personality illness that is deeply resistant to therapy. His endless criticism of me never ceased. I was reduced to cook, maid, errand girl, and more recently, farm hand. That's all I was. That's all I was worth to him. This is a very painful reality.

I was forced to tell our son, Marc, that his father wanted to divorce me. Larry couldn't and didn't tell Marc. He has probably known all along that some day he would muster enough courage to divorce me for his "secret life".

Why didn't we at least move near his family in Oregon? **Why Washington? We know no one here, and his job wasn't even here.** As usual, my opinion did not matter. He said we would buy it now, and in a few years, we would retire here. This was his excuse for commuting to Las Vegas from here, shuttle to PDX, courtesy of me, for the first year. Then he was able to transfer to Seattle with his company, where he began renting a room during the weekdays. After talking with locals here, they told me that Chehalis/Centralia are mid-point cities between Seattle and Portland, where many gays meet in local hotels. So now the move here finally made sense! He wanted to be close to Seattle AND Portland. I searched on the internet for Portland's tourist info and found *www.travelportland.com/visitors/tours.html.* I noticed on the left of the website was a link called "Gay Portland". I clicked on it, and one of the slogans on the page was, "Keep Portland Queer". Well, my gay husband is doing his part to keep their city queer, all right!

Most weekends he drove home. I wonder what his employer thought of his constant requests for moving! Larry told me in October 2006 that HIS JOB wanted him to move to

ABQ, by Jan. 1, 2007. I called his boss and found out that this supposedly mandated move to ABQ was at LARRY'S REQUEST! Later I found out that his "boy toy" lives in ABQ. Obviously, he got mad that I had called his boss. This was my first task at my new job as detective.

But instead of moving to ABQ, he got his boss to agree to allow him to work part-time (with a pending divorce) from his residence, now in Portland. He requested this because his father, who lives in Salem, is terminally ill, and he wanted to live close to his father for a while. So why didn't he move to Salem? Well now we know! Portland has the gay life, not Salem! Even though during our marriage, I asked him if he wanted to go to his father's place, for Christmas, and he said, "No." I asked why, and he said, "I don't want to go there." So now he wants to LIVE near him? Huh! If nothing makes sense in your life, HE'S GAY!!!

I wonder now how many other moves have we made unnecessarily? In 1993 when we lived in ABQ, Larry knew he would be a top-contender for making the rank of full colonel, because Larry worked with a general who Larry thought surely would and could promote him. Then at Larry's request, we moved to Saudi Arabia. Why? I didn't know. When the review board met, while we lived in Saudi, Larry did NOT make full colonel. The general in Saudi was unable to grant Larry the promotion. Tell me, why would Larry want to move to Saudi when he knew that if he stayed in ABQ, chances would be excellent to make full colonel? Nothing EVER made sense, living in this fraudulent marriage! There had to have been a reason for him to leave ABQ; one that I will probably never know.

Marc, our son, is a wonderfully compassionate young man, whose personality, and behavior are a result of my_efforts alone. Marc never connected to Larry, due to Larry's lack of presence and effort with him. Larry told Marc on one occasion, "I know it doesn't SEEM like I love you, but I do." When a parent is absent MOST of the time, it is very hard to have a relationship of any kind, and expect the child to be well adjusted. Marc told me that he didn't FEEL Larry's love. After I told Marc about the divorce, he emailed Larry and said, "Why are you doing this? I can't concentrate. My grades have gone way down. I'm so depressed." Larry replied, "I do care. I just wished everyone else cared too." What a narcissist! Marc was looking for compassion. He only heard a selfish remark from his father!

How I Found Him Out

After living in "the fog" of unreality for two months, trying to make sense of why Larry wanted to divorce me, and internalizing the blame because that's just the way he made me feel all along, I made my discovery. It was in early December 2006. I was able to have a copy of his cell phone records mailed to me. I HATED to have to play detective. Marriage is SUPPOSED to be based on trust. I always thought that he wouldn't lie to me, since I TRUSTED him. I have never lied to him! I called one particular number from ABQ, NM that stood out, and got a message recording which said, "Hi, This is Steven..." I confronted Larry, and asked him how many Stevens have there been? He looked right at me, and said, "None of your business." In a legal document, Larry wrote, "I have recently admitted to myself and to my family that I am a gay man." He never admitted anything to me, our grown daughter, or to our son except in this document. In fact, I never received the truth, understanding, OR an apology for any of his actions during our marriage. I don't believe he would have EVER told me the truth on his own. Yet I know that I _deserved_ his honesty.

Sex Tells It All

Well, I REALLY let him off the hook easy on this one! It was below my personal dignity to beg for sex. Actually, we stopped having sex soon after my son was born. Even though I didn't know what Larry was doing behind my back, how can you help but not "feel" it? Call it woman's intuition, but I knew something wasn't right. I knew I didn't love him any more because of the way he made me feel – finding many faults with me and my family, discounting my opinion on everything, just his "authoritative" personality – never nurturing or compassionate, so I really didn't want sex with this person that he had become. He couldn't even hug me. Once in a while I'd give him a hug, and he inflated himself, making his chest hard, and gave me a side-hug. His kisses were mechanical as sex had been with him all along. I think about the "oldies" song called "The Shoo-op Song." It goes like this: "If you wanna know, if he loves you so, it's in his kiss – that's where it is." Occasionally I see other couples holding hands and this serves as a reminder of what my hopes and dreams were for married life. I have been **cheated** of all of this. My gay husband robbed me of my dreams, and he doesn't care. I feel the rape of 28 years times 365 days = 10,220 times, to my inner self!

The Truth Behind His Lies

I have lost who I am in this marriage as I tried so hard at solving the insolvable. I believe that he thought that my role in life was to serve him and our children in exchange for his meeting my most basic physical needs like food and shelter. What I will never understand is how Larry destroyed my life, yet he continues to be angry with me. I simply don't get it! His logic is so twisted!

This has not been a marriage. It has been fraud. After finding out his secret, it doesn't change the years of emotional neglect or abuse I have experienced, but it does explain it. Last spring he wanted to plant 100 more blueberry plants, and he showed me how to make the rows for planting them by hand using a hoe. I walked away. He got mad. I didn't care any more. I guess I became numb and dealt with it. I was so totally resigned to life without love and affection. I was not educated at all about gay men; I never thought I had to be because who would have thought that a gay man would have any interest in a woman!

Now I understand that it is because some gay men prey on anyone they think they can manipulate. They think that your

30

misery is their pleasure. It "justifies" them somehow. Many more SHOCKING realizations came to mind AFTER I realized that I have only been his "mock" wife. An example was when he had me sign a waiver when he retired to waive my rights to military survivor benefit insurance. He said he'd have insurance for me, <u>and I trusted him</u>!

This sick and diabolical person was content to keep the truth from me all-the-while being too selfish to understand what love is. He stayed married until our children were grown, only to blind-side me now. The realization that this man took me as his wife because he was too cowardly to go through life the way that he should--as a gay man--has been indescribably traumatic! So now after investing years of my life trying to make the best of a bad marriage, I am now faced with the nightmare of having to start over. I am still unable to concentrate. I'd like to know how long before I can stop incessantly playing the broken record in my head that holds me prisoner every waking moment since I first discovered that 'he's gay!'

It has been six months now for me, and I only have momentary reprieves of other thoughts in my waking hours. Sometimes I just want to scream if one more person tells me it is time to move on with my life. I know I have to move on, but it is a constant struggle. I often feel paralyzed and am still deeply saddened. For the last eight months, I've cried almost every day, living in a daze of disbelief and going through the motions of living, still in a state of confusion and depression.

The best years of my life have passed in front of my eyes— years where I could have been living a life without deceit, contempt, rejection, and abuse. And now I look around and realize that I can't get back what I have lost – 28 years! If I would have had a true partner from the beginning, a man who was nurturing and supportive, rather than a man who was just standing in as a husband, who knows where my life would be now. It's just tragic. Larry stole my life and soul and he did it without thought, notice, or especially remorse!

Knowing that Larry has been hiding his true identity has left me with an inability to trust my judgment because it has destroyed my own sense of being able to make decisions. I keep asking myself how I could have been so blind... stupid... misled. I start to wonder what else happened in my life that was an illusion. My husband didn't "appear" gay, but yet he was!

And so now Larry's in a big hurry to lead his new life, while I'm still trying to recover from the news. And I'M THE ONE STUCK ON HIS FARM now, while he has begun living **his** "new" life. I, too, would like to be able to move on and reclaim my life, my soul, and my inner peace. Unlike Larry, however, I feel that this will take me many years. Not only have I lost 28 years with Larry, but many more to come for my recovery.

It's difficult to think of myself as not being defined by his criticism - not as someone who isn't as perfect as he thought I should be. This is a new way of life for sure, but a much healthier one. I hope that one day the pain will be gone.

❖

PROFILE #3: SALLY T. - 58, Texas, married 31 years, divorced five years, two children, departmental secretary at a university.

Red Flags

Looking back to my years growing up, I cannot remember ever discussing or even knowing anyone who was gay. I grew up in a small community of cotton farmers in West Texas and was very isolated from the real world and especially from such issues.

I met my husband at a university after graduating from high school. We had a wonderful relationship and marriage for about seven years. We had two beautiful daughters. I had no clue there was a problem and thought I had the perfect husband and life.

Our sex life began to change after our second daughter was born. He became distant as well, and I remember crying at night because he never came to bed with me and he would stay up late. I rarely had any of his attention. His excuses at that time were that he was taking care of our older daughter because I needed to be with the baby. He also told me that we fight so much that he didn't feel like making love.

He became very depressed and complained about his unhappiness with his job. We had been married 17 years when he decided to transfer to another city. His depression had become worse and I thought this was a good idea. He moved into an apartment to start his new job and I waited behind for our house to sell. It took about six months for the house to sell and he had still not found a house for us to move into. The girls and I moved into an apartment waiting for him to find a house in the new city. Not long after that, he announced to me that he was unhappy in the city that he had moved to and he felt that the girls and I would be very unhappy there as well. The city was large, the traffic was horrible, and he wanted us to stay behind. He gave the excuse that the schools were better here and he would travel home on weekends, which resulted in him coming home about every three weeks or longer.

We began our long distance marriage, and I was very unhappy. He came home less and less. I cried so much that even today the girls remember my crying more than anything else. He said he loved me and didn't want a divorce and we remained in the marriage for 14 more years.

As I look back, there were years of depression for him. He seldom came home. He was unwilling to find us a house. I believed everything he told me, and I believed all of his excuses. Even later as more red flags appeared, I continued to ignore them. I was depressed as well and could never figure out why he wouldn't or couldn't talk to me.

He found a roommate to save money and moved in with another man. As the years went by, I accidentally found out that this roommate was gay. Our sex life became more and more non-existent and he preferred positions where he couldn't see my face, which now makes more sense to me. I never caught on to that before either.

To add to the misery, I asked him several times if he were gay. He denied it and was disgusted that I would think such a thing. He asked me once why I thought that, and I told him that it would make more sense.

Even though the red flags were everywhere, some of them alone would not indicate that a person is gay. If you put them together, I think you would see clearly that he had a deep dark secret. Keeping that in mind, I thought it would be a good idea to just list as many as I could think of, but remember my husband was not home much. The list included:

✓ Determination to go out with the boys at least once a week (he met his partner during this time)
✓ Around age 30, he began tanning and working out
✓ My daughters remember him laying out to get a tan in a Speedo
✓ He lost interest in kissing
✓ He lost interest in holding hands or showing any affection
✓ His not having an interest in sex, making excuses
✓ His not looking me in the face during sex
✓ His wanting the behind position
✓ His having trouble having and keeping an erection
✓ He would not perform oral sex
✓ His not wanting his family to move out of town with him
✓ His not wanting his family to come to visit him in the other city
✓ His making excuses that the house he lived in belong to his roommate and he didn't feel comfortable with us coming in to stay
✓ His treating me like another daughter, no intimacy
✓ His avoided coming home if his daughters weren't going to be there
✓ He avoided being with me during possible times alone
✓ His refusing to talk and answer questions
✓ He got upset and mad and left if I asked him what he was hiding
✓ He could not sleep and stayed up smoking when he did come home

- ✓ His depression
- ✓ He had some OCD (Obsessive Compulsive Disorder) such as had to have clean cars at all times, wanted a clean house, was a neat dresser, etc.
- ✓ He was interested in design and decorating
- ✓ He chose everything for a house we built (carpet, wallpaper, counter tops, etc.)
- ✓ His never accepting any blame for any of our problems
- ✓ He didn't mind shopping with all females
- ✓ He liked to shop and help pick out clothes for his kids and me
- ✓ He denied that we ever communicated well during our marriage
- ✓ I found out his roommate was gay *
- ✓ He decided to retire and not move back home *
- ✓ His family was not invited to his retirement party *

*FINALLY registered and I eventually filed for a divorce

Blame Was the Name of His Game

My ex had a way of turning things around on me. If I complained about him not ever making love to me, he would tell me that we were always fighting, and he just didn't feel like making love when we are mad at each other. Many times he would just fall asleep in his recliner and not come to bed until very late.

I never got along with his mother, and he sided with her anytime there was an argument. We had a big argument one Christmas because she felt we should come on Christmas day, and not afterwards. We had two families to go see, and she was always demanding priority. My ex asked me one year to leave my parents early to go see her, and he would tell her that Christmas was over on the 26th and we would just leave. He seemed upset with her and I agreed. Leaving on the 26th and him saying anything to her never happened. It was all forgotten because he did not want to bring it up and ruin the holiday. He was furious when I exploded and told them both

35

what I thought. I believe she knew for years about her son being gay. I was blamed for that awful Christmas and how I acted.

Throughout our marriage, I was to blame for anything that went wrong. During the divorce, he did not want to let me keep the house, and he told me that he could force me to sell it and we would divide the equity. He did not want me bringing in another man to live in HIS house. He also told me that I favored my family and he hated to go see them, and I never wanted to go see his. This was quite funny to me since he and our daughters loved going to see my parents. My mother adored him and my family liked him. My mother often cooked his favorites instead of mine! He had supported her many times during her difficulties she faced with her own parents and siblings.

Our daughters loved going to the farm and enjoyed seeing their cousins when they would visit. My ex had no siblings to visit; it was just he and his mother. To this day, he has never acknowledged any blame.

Perhaps not being in the same town and in the same house, I was one of the lucky ones. I didn't have constant abuse from him directly. I felt alone but I stayed busy and didn't allow myself to think about the real problems. I didn't turn to drugs or alcohol, and I didn't feel the need to seek therapy. I certainly knew he would never go for counseling. I have felt very sad for wasting so many years of my life with this marriage.

Happily Ever After – For Real

After the divorce, we stayed friends for a few years and then he admitted he was gay in an email about three years later. I became angry and decided to be mad for a year. During that time I never dated and had no love interest at all. Even though I knew he was gay, hearing it from him was a shock and I became determined to talk and write about my life, hoping to help others.

An old classmate from high school asked me out on a date last year and we became very close. I began realizing I could love and be happy again. He made me realize that there is life after being married to a gay man, and I will always appreciate what he did for me.

I am searching for my true soul mate, and I believe I will find him. I am a happier person for moving on and not feeling sorry for myself.

I am a happy and positive person now, and you can be too. Just believe in yourself and know that none of this was ever your fault.

PROFILE #4: Charlotte M., North Carolina, married 30 years, divorced 18 years, one son and one daughter both professionals.

Red Flags

I was a naive 20-year-old virgin when I married my ex. We had a long distance romance mainly by letter back in the 1950s. I had arrived from overseas for a two-year stay and I am still here. He was very charming and a professional, and I was impressed. We were married six months after our first meeting.

He was thirty and I thought that was strange as most guys were married before then.

We tried to have sex once before the wedding, but it was a disaster; he said it would be best to wait. On the honeymoon I was miserable and had nightmares about rats under the bed. We were very uncomfortable with one another but I thought that would get better. It never did. I became pregnant almost right away and then had a second child 21 months later. He kicked me in my back when I was pregnant the second time. I was really depressed after the birth and things just kept going downhill from then on. I told him I wanted to go back to Europe and he said that I could go but the children would stay with him. I did not argue and stuck it out for years until the children went to college. I then thought sex would be better and looked forward to time together. But that was not the case. When I got back from a weekend trip to the coast he had moved out of the bedroom saying his snoring was keeping me awake. So there was no sex for the last few years of our marriage.

It all came to a head when a co-worker of mine told me that my husband had accosted her son, who worked for him. Of course he had not mentioned this to me. I told him I needed to talk to him and he finally came clean and did not apologize. I discovered later that he is a pedophile who likes 16-year-old boys. He admitted to sleeping with one and that he had affairs in service and in college. He blamed his family for being molested by siblings and had known since age eight that he was gay.

As you can imagine I was horrified by the trouble he had caused his employees and their parents. None ever complained to me. It is true that the wife is always the last to know. At the same time I was so relieved because for the first time in thirty years, I knew it was not my fault .He had always given me the impression that there was something wrong with me.

He lives a couple of hours away from me. We do not speak. My children keep in touch with him. Neither of them has children, and I wonder if their Dad is the reason. The really sad thing is that he is a homophobic homosexual who is now a lonely old man. He is lucky that he was not taken to court. I learned later that one mother almost did file charges but she did not want her son to go through the trauma.

I mostly have gone on with my life and have had a few relationships but nothing serious. I mostly do not think about it anymore but like now it all comes flooding back.

PROFILE #5:   Bethany S., Texas, married three years, divorced two years, one child, Teacher

Red Flags – Signs I Missed

When I first met my husband Mabrey in 2003, I remember thinking, "Wow! I can't believe he's single." He was a tall, handsome, friendly, church-going great guy. He was divorced from his first wife and had two children. He had been married ten years and divorced nearly two years when we met. I remember thinking that he was "out of my league." I had just recently gotten divorced and thought I wasn't possibly good enough for him. People always ask me, "Didn't you see the signs?" But no, I truly didn't. Looking back, of course, hindsight is 20/20, and now I totally see all of the red flags/missed signs that were so recognizable. But, at the time, it is truly the furthest thing from your mind. You are completely, genuinely not even entertaining any thoughts about the man you are dating being 'gay.'

I wasn't too alarmed that my husband didn't hunt, fish, golf, or play sports...some men aren't into those things. But, he didn't even like to watch any sports. So much so that he set the favorites channels setup on the TV's in our house to skip all of the sports networks completely. Normally if a woman walks through the den on a Saturday and her husband is on the couch watching television, he's watching a sporting event. Mine would watch the "gingerbread cookie baking contest" on the Food Network. I always said, "He was a great girlfriend-just not a husband." He loved to go shopping with me and was a great 'girlfriend' type companion. He was extremely vain – staring into the mirrors a lot – constantly grooming himself. He hated the hair on his back, and he would go and get it waxed off. Once he even had his eyebrows waxed. He loved pedicures and manicures too. When he would sit, he'd cross his legs like a woman. He was very animated while talking and full of lively conversation. He loved visiting with the ladies in the neighborhood too – totally fit right in with 'girl' talk.

I was extremely naïve and didn't realize till much later that in fact, my husband had only married me to keep up the presumption of being a heterosexual male – with a wife and child, etc. I truly believe he never did love me. To him, I was just what he needed; a single, hardworking, educated professional from a good family that could offer the perfect 'front' for him. My sister told me, a year later, that the first time she and her husband had met Mabrey that they turned to each other and asked, "Do you think he's gay?" I remember when I told my father that Mabrey was gay, he responded with, "Well, that doesn't surprise me." No one seemed to be surprised. It's like everyone knew and saw all of the red flags, except for me.

Blame Was the Name of His Game

Being blamed unfairly by your husband for his being gay is one of the hardest things. It truly does a number on your self-esteem. My husband was a very negative person, constantly putting me down. Nothing about me or anything I did was right. It was always my fault. He always made me feel as if I was never pretty enough, skinny enough, smart enough. He did everything he could to belittle me and blame me unfairly for his depression and sadness for not being able to live authentically and be honest about who he was.

At the time when your husband is blaming you, you do truly believe that it's your fault. Looking back, it is ridiculous to think about how I believed for a second any excuse he gave me. But while you are living it, you take it hook, line and sinker – and allow it to chisel away at your self-esteem piece by piece until you feel no self-worth. It's a little embarrassing to admit now the excuses he gave – that I actually believed – but it's important that I share openly so other women in my position will realize how ridiculous the blame game can be.

While we dated, my husband and I shared passionate French kisses, just like most couples do. Literally the night after we were married – the French kissing stopped – completely. He never would French kiss again, never. I mean seriously, no open mouth whatsoever. He just puckered lips closed for a peck on the lips or cheek from that moment forward. Of course I found this extremely odd. I would try to kiss him passionately, but his lips would remain closed tightly. Finally after numerous embarrassing attempts, I asked him why he would not French kiss me anymore. He replied, "Well, it's because you have bad breath." I reminded him that I had tried to French kiss him numerous days/times and he wasn't willing. How could my breath be a problem when he'd never mentioned it before, ever? He again said that I had bad breath and with that he never, ever, ever French kissed me again.

Basically from that moment forward the only type of kiss I got was a quick, tight-lipped, 'peck' on the cheek. Then if I begged for a kiss on the lips, it was a quick, tight-lipped, 'peck' on the lips – with both of our lips closed.

Sex Tells It All

I have always considered myself a very sexual, loving, affectionate woman. I always enjoyed intimacy, especially in the context of an intimate, loving relationship. I had always hoped to be in a marriage where my husband enjoyed making love to me. There was obviously some chemistry when I met my husband and we enjoyed what I thought was a normal, dating relationship. When we married, our sex life changed almost instantly – or should I say almost 'ended' instantly. It was so bizarre. My husband immediately began making excuses why he would not even sleep in the same bed or room with me. He said that it was because I snored at night.

That was his excuse – it was all my fault. I snored, so he started sleeping in the guest bedroom, and we didn't have sex. If I would ask him to come to bed with me, make love, then he could go sleep in the guest room there was always another excuse; he had a 'stomach ache' or a 'headache' or he was 'too tired'-- all the classic excuses. He even started blaming me more – trying to make me feel bad – saying that I had too strong of a sexual appetite that he just couldn't satisfy. I was thinking, "A strong sexual appetite – are you kidding? I'm only asking for sex a minimum of once a month – we're newlyweds." It was so bizarre. I was made to feel like some sex addict while he never cared to have sex again. It made me question myself and feel guilty for asking him for intimacy.

How I Caught Him

I was nine months pregnant and two weeks before delivering our baby. My husband had me sleeping in the guest bedroom that summer, since he couldn't sleep with me in my 'condition.' I was up and down to the bathroom while he needed his rest for work each day. Besides, we had slept in separate bedrooms since we married because he said I snored and he couldn't sleep with me. Sometimes when I would wake up in the night to go to the bathroom, I would see his bedroom light on from down the hall. If I walked in and saw him at the computer, he immediately would jump and click 'home' to get off the webpage he was on. The next day I decided to get online on the computer and see if the 'history' would tell me what website he was on when I walked in late at night. In my thoughts I remember dreading finding out he was looking at pornography – naked women or men/women having sex. Boy was I in for a surprise… I would have loved to have only seen naked women on the website he was viewing – instead it was only naked men in sex acts with each other. My jaw dropped. I couldn't believe what I was looking at. Surely this was an "accident" and not something he looked at intentionally. Not my husband… the one who never kissed me or wanted sex…The one who never participated in any sports, hunting, fishing or golfing. Not him – how could this be?

As I studied the history on the computer Internet, I was so shocked to see that night after night, for hours – he was viewing totally gay pornography online. He obviously didn't know about the "clear history" choice on the computer. I was able to see days, weeks and months back of all his viewing. I wrote down all the different website addresses – there were probably about 30 to 40 different ones. I wrote down the dates, times, and for how long he viewed each website. Some of the websites required paid subscriptions. WOW! Can you imagine, two weeks from delivering our baby and I am sitting at the computer viewing this – realizing that my husband is obviously "gay." However, I knew that if I confronted him that night he would simply deny it and claim it was a one-time mistake. So, I decided to clear the history myself (after recording everything on paper) and pretend I knew nothing. I pretended that nothing was wrong or that I had found out anything.

Each night I would say good night to him, I'd go to the guest bedroom and he in the master bedroom with the computer – all the while knowing he'd be up viewing his gay porn. Each day after he'd go to work I'd log online, view the history from the night before, record the website addresses, times, hours he viewed, and then clear the history again. I did this everyday for two months. I knew then that I had plenty of proof that this was not an accident, and I was ready to confront him.

We had a two-month old baby. I was on maternity leave, a brand new mommy, and breast-feeding. He lost his job, and I would have to cut short my maternity leave to go back to teaching to support us. I told him that I needed to talk with him that night and that he shouldn't waste any time trying to lie or deny anything – that what I was about to ask him about I had proof was something he'd been doing awhile and not an accident. I did that because I simply wanted to avoid the lies and denial. I wanted to cut to the chase. When I told him what I had realized that he'd been doing, and what I'd been tracking and recording for months; I simply asked him; "Why?" His first answer in response was "curiosity." I told him that curiosity is something that someone typically satisfies within a quick time period, not months and months of re-viewing something. I told him I knew that was a lie – it wasn't because he was "curious." His next reply was that it was a "fantasy." I realized that obviously he is being honest now and truthfully telling me he 'fantasizes' about naked men and sex acts with men…homosexuality. I asked him how long he'd been doing this and he admitted about three years. I asked him if he had already acted on his fantasy and had sex with another man and he said no.

At that point, I wasn't sure whether he was lying or telling the truth. My husband had lied to me so many times in our short marriage that it had become very hard to believe him. I guess I'll never know truly if he had already had sex with another man at that point in his life or not. If he hadn't, he surely did want too and was killing himself by hiding in the closet. My husband would not come out and admit or say the words, "I'm gay," but I knew he was deep in denial and living in the closet. At that point, he probably had not admitted to himself that he was gay.

I told him that since we had a new baby, I was a new mom, breastfeeding and needing to wean our child and go back to work early since he lost his job, that we would have to just 'table' this for now. Basically I was juggling all the plates that I could and wasn't physically, emotionally or spiritually able to confront his 'gayness' at that moment in time. I told him we would table it and go to counseling the next summer when school was out. We agreed to continue to sleep in separate bedrooms, like we had since we married, and simply pretend – for now – that everything was ok. He loved that – pretending – he was quite good at it. He'd been pretending his entire adult life.

He wanted to stay married and continue to keep up the front at church, work, with friends, by having a wife and new baby – how could anyone suspect he was gay? He wanted us to raise our child together and just pretend to the world that we were a happy, normal couple. For me, it was very depressing and draining – living a lie – everyday knowing that my husband down the hall is gay. It was like living with your guy cousin – but worse – because I was so angry with him for being gay and being the cause of the demise of our marriage. When the summer arrived I scheduled counseling for us to meet this homosexuality issue head on. To my surprise, the counselor basically turned things around to ask me, "What would be wrong if your husband is gay?" Then my husband started private counseling with the counselor. I was left completely frustrated with zero self-esteem again feeling like I was to blame. It was so hard to try and continue on living this lie with my husband day to day.

By Christmas I decided that I wanted him to leave and wanted a divorce. I basically realized that I would rather be lonely alone then in a marriage to a gay man while allowing him to use our child and me as his props to appear heterosexual. I also thought about what it would be like when our child started kindergarten someday and mentioned "Mommy's room," and "Daddy's room," and how that would affect her. I also realized that it was horrible for her to grow up seeing a Mommy and Daddy who never touched, hugged, kissed or were in love. I didn't want her to think that is what love is and that it was a loving, normal relationship when parents don't share a bedroom. I decided I had to do what was best for our child and me and divorce him.

Happily Ever After – For Real!

Happily Ever After for me has been not dealing with the constant negativity and tearing away at my self-esteem by being married to a husband who is such a coward and cannot be honest with himself and live an authentic life. No, I have not moved on in regards to dating or relationships whatsoever. In fact, I haven't dated at all.

My concentration has been on trying to regain my self-esteem and be the best single parent-working Mom I can be to my toddler. It's taking a long time to feel like I can finally truly talk about what has happened with my marriage. I pray that in the future I will begin to love myself and heal from the wounds this ordeal caused. I don't regret meeting/marrying my husband, because I wouldn't have my precious beloved child if it weren't for him. However, that is truly the only good thing that came from our union.

PROFILE #6: PATRICIA P., 58, Illinois, divorced, on disability. I am an only child. My father was an angry alcoholic, and my mother suffered from depression all of her life with two suicide attempts as far as I know. She also suffered from OCD, washing her hands countless times a day. Their Draconian drama was a battle for control. They played off one another like Laurel and Hardy except that it wasn't amusing. I spent all of my childhood with a knot in my stomach and walking on eggshells because I never knew who was going to drop the day's bomb first. One thing my parents did agree on was that they wanted a boy instead of a girl. Early on, I learned to put the FUN in dysfunctional or else go out of my mind.

I have been married twice, and both marriages ended in divorce. The first ended because he had an affair and the second because I was on the rebound and married the wrong man for the wrong reasons.

My father was Catholic. My mother was Jewish, but her family converted to Christianity in Germany (massacres and all). She attended a Lutheran church. I was raised Catholic but left the church in my 20's. Today, I am a non-denominational Christian and have been for about 15 years.

Red Flags - Signs I Missed

I first met Chuck when we were both sophomores in high school. There didn't appear to be anything gay about him at that time. But then, I didn't even know what "gay" was. After graduation we went our separate ways. He found me after 39 years after tracking me down on the Internet. He didn't know it, but for all those years I was still in love with him. We were not married; we lived together. In retrospect, the signs were everywhere:

✓ He told me hadn't had sex "with a woman" in 18 years. I thought it was strange but, of course, rationalized that he was a man of high moral certitude. Yeah, right.
✓ He has a brother who is gay. This is important since homosexuality tends to run in families.
✓ He spoke like a hard-core homophobe, pontificating that homosexuality was a choice and that gays would burn in hell.
✓ He deified his mother and his daughter to the point of extreme.
✓ He had an overall negative view of other women. In fact, I would say he was a misogynist.

✓ He had no interest in sex with me.
✓ He paraded me in front of his family and friends like a trophy, repeatedly telling them that I was the only woman who could love him.
✓ He constantly contradicted himself.
✓ He claimed to have a "special" relationship with God in which God supposedly excused his behavior. That behavior entailed bashing and trashing me as a woman and as a human being.
✓ He was secretive, angry and depressed. Oh look, he was actually my parents!

Sex Tells It All

Or should I say, "No sex tells it all?" The following are the reasons Chuck would give me for not wanting sex:

✓ Premarital sex was a sin worthy of eternal damnation.
✓ He did not find me attractive.
✓ All I thought about was sex.
✓ His stomach was upset.
✓ His intestines were abnormal.
✓ His ears hurt.
✓ His back hurt.
✓ His instep was off balance.
✓ There were demons in the neighborhood.
✓ He had a sore throat.
✓ He was busy thinking.
✓ His sinuses were clogged.
✓ He wanted to sleep in his recliner.

On the handful of occasions that Chuck tried to exhibit what I can only call sexual charity, he failed miserably. He could not maintain an erection long enough to have intercourse. Even if he could have intercourse, he only wanted to enter me from behind. He did not want to see my face. Sex, to him, was just that - it was sex with no intimacy. The most sex we ever had was me masturbating him. Yes, it was all about him. He was not in the least bit interested in giving me pleasure.

How I Caught Him

Chuck had been spending more and more time away from home. Come on, it doesn't take five hours to buy a power cord at Radio Shack. One morning he went to extreme lengths to get himself all dolled up because he was "having a watch battery replaced." He smelled like a whorehouse. As he was leaving, I asked him if he was seeing someone else. Of course, he denied it. He didn't return until about seven hours later. He bought me a present. It was a huge, framed print of a portion of the Serenity Prayer:

God grant me the serenity
to accept the things I cannot change;
courage to change the things I can;
and wisdom to know the difference.

He made a big production of how he had to spend all day hunting high and low for the perfect gift for me. I knew he was lying. This was a man who thought he splurged when he once bought me a $3.00 nozzle can of something resembling cheese.

I asked him why he bought the Serenity Prayer for me. He said it was because he wasn't going to change, that he only wanted a brother-sister relationship with me, and that I needed to accept it.

All of a sudden it hit me like a ton of bricks. I said, "You're gay like your brother, aren't you?" He just smirked at me and said he was. He became belligerent and told me he didn't care what I or anybody else thought of it. He went so far as to say he was proud of it. He claimed that I drove him further into homosexuality, that it was my fault. When I asked him if he was having sex with other men, he said he could not imagine being homosexual and not having sex. He then laughed at me for being so naïve.

48

Chuck left that night. He only took his personal papers. I have not seen him since.

The Truth Behind the Lies

When I asked Chuck why he called me in the first place, why he moved in with me and why all the deception, he told me that he thought I would be able to rehabilitate him into being straight, but I had failed. Chuck had, unbeknownst to me, placed a burden on me that I would never be able to carry. He had expected me to be his Messiah.

I had been suffering from major depression when Chuck came back into my life. By the time he left I was emotionally paralyzed. In addition, the stress triggered the onset of Celiac Disease which is irreversible. I was my own victim as well. I fell for his lies hook, line and sinker. The Cinderella in me made Chuck her Prince Charming, a role which he could never, ever play, at least with a female.

Happily Ever After - For Real

It's not "happily after all" for me, not yet. I sunk about as low as I could. My self esteem was in the gutter, and I'm still clawing my way up. How could I allow this to happen? I loved him, and love can sometimes trick the mind. It's like being on drugs.

If Chuck had been honest about his homosexuality in the beginning, I really do believe we would have had a fine relationship as friends. But he was on a desperate downward spiral and had no qualms about taking me along for the ride. What he did was unconscionable and without excuse. The same goes for me. I had no right to allow myself to be emotionally abused, to make excuses for my abuser and to forfeit my self respect.

PROFILE #7: NANCY D. I live in Cooper City, Florida, a suburb of Fort Lauderdale. I met my husband when I was 18 years old and in college. He was my first true love. We dated for two years before we married. We had two children; Eric, 22 years old, and Amy, 18 years old. We separated after 23 years of marriage, and divorced three and a half years later. The divorce took a long time because of one major complication: my ex-husband and I own a business together. Yes, we do have to work together and see each other every day. That is something with which I am currently struggling and haven't quite found a solution to yet! Now my story…

Red Flags – Signs I Missed

I have to admit that I had absolutely no idea that my husband was gay until the moment he told me, after 23 years of marriage. No one that I have spoken to that knew him ever recognized it either. However, I do want to offer one cautionary note. Shortly before we were married, we were discussing our sexual histories. Mine was limited to him, so that was a short conversation for me! He told me that he had had sex "one time" with a male teaching assistant during college. He told me it was "gross" and that it was just experimental sex.

Since it was the 1970's, I dismissed it as part of the open world we were living in at the time. I don't think I ever thought about that conversation again until he came out. However, after speaking to several straight men since then, I would offer this piece of advice: almost all men, if they are straight, will have NO desire to have sex with another man and will NOT choose to have sex with another man. They are really into having sex with women, but men? No way. So, that was my "red flag" and I totally missed it. Don't let it happen to you!

Blame Was (and Is) the Name of His Game

My ex-husband has a very difficult time taking responsibility for the choices and actions he has taken since before he met me, which was AFTER he realized he was gay. *Perhaps that is a family trait, because shortly after he gave me the "big news," he also told me that his brother, an educated 52-year-old, reacted in this way when he heard about my ex's homosexuality: "Well, if Nancy had been a better wife, none of this would have ever happened." Can you imagine? What power I must wield to actually turn someone gay! Of course, wouldn't you think that I would also have the power to then make him straight again? I find it truly pathetic that not only did my brother-in-law say this, but also that my ex felt the need to share that with me!*

One of the cruelest things **my ex** has done to me since he came out has been to continuously blame me for the failure of the marriage. He has said over and over again that the failure of our marriage was either: (A) totally my fault because I am a "f___ing bitch" or (B) just as much my fault as his and that his being gay had nothing to do with it. I think that he believes that if he says it enough times, it will become true! I am so offended by both of these statements because it is so clear that a homosexual has no business marrying a heterosexual. It will never work. How could either person's emotional needs, let alone sexual needs, ever be met in such a relationship?

The whole time I was working on our relationship, I was under the impression that we were building it on a foundation of concrete, while the entire time my ex knew we were building it on quicksand! And how he watched me work, work, work away at it, trying everything in my power to make him happy and, in turn, me happy. I find that truly abusive. It is simply one more aspect of how much he tried to force ME to carry the blame for the failure of our marriage and our family, and unfortunately, how often I was willing to carry it.

I still struggle internally because it is my nature to take responsibility for things that happen in my life, but I have come to realize that this one just wasn't my doing. As I've said jokingly, but it's really the truth, the one thing I did "wrong" was to not have the "correct equipment", and that, my friends, is truly NOT my fault!

Sex *Doesn't* Tell It All

In my case, there's not much to say about our sex life. It was fairly normal, with him usually wanting it more than I did. It wasn't the most exciting sex in the world, but, since he was my first, I had nothing to compare it to. I will say that he had NO problem performing, which does make me wonder if perhaps he's actually bi-sexual. I have met gay men that would run screaming if they saw a vagina, but that wasn't my ex at all. Unless he was doing the greatest acting job since Laurence Olivier, I have to believe that, at least for 30 years of his life, he was bi. He, of course, denies this, but it's the only thing that makes sense to me.

The Truth Behind His Lies

I can't honestly say that I know the entire truth about my ex's life throughout our marriage, and that's because I don't want to know. Right after he told me he was gay, he said to me, "Didn't you notice when we were on all those cruises that I was checking out all the guys in their bathing suits?" I stopped him right there and told him not to dare ruin all of my wonderful memories of our many cruise vacations. Many of them were with our kids!

Of course, now I do realize that when the kids and I would go back to the cabin at night and he went to the "casino," he probably wasn't at the casino at all! Those are the kinds of thoughts that make me both very angry and very sad. I try very hard to avoid them, but they do creep in. I'm sure that there were many nights that he told me he was working late as a cover for what he was really doing.

I know for a fact that he was engaging in unsafe sex with men while we were married because he was tested after he told me was gay. And, boy, does that make me mad! He put MY health at risk! I honestly don't think I will ever forgive that. I also know that he was enjoying himself in gay chat rooms because a high school friend, whom I had not spoken to in literally 30 years, called me after he figured out that it was my ex chatting with HIM on line! Fortunately, this occurred after I already knew the truth, but it paints quite the picture....me sitting in the family room with the kids, while he was in the den entertaining himself on line!

I value truth so very much, and it pains me deeply to know that I spent so many years of my life with a liar. I always thought we shared the belief that honesty was the best policy, but clearly only ONE of us felt that way! I know it hurts my kids a lot too. They see the hypocrisy in his espousing the importance of honesty to them when they were growing up, while he was lying to them on a daily basis. I have no idea how he can live with himself after the damage he has done, but I guess he manages by blaming the whole thing on others—especially me.

I would also like to mention that I don't believe he was ready to come out when he did. I asked him several probing questions about his therapy never dreaming that THIS would be the answer, which led to his breaking down in tears and 'fessing up. I'm not sure he ever would have come out, although his surliness and lack of affection towards me became increasingly obvious. I guess he needed to be pushed into it. Perhaps I should be calling him the Cowardly Lion.

Happily Ever After – For Real!

I have moved on in many ways, and that has taken a lot of hard work (and therapy) on my part. I won't tell you it's easy. There is so much hurt, anger, and grief to deal with, and, yes, they are all still there. I really thought I had the rest of my life pretty much worked out and then – BOOM – I found out that everything I thought was going to happen was NOT going to happen. The person I trusted the most became the person I trusted the least. Those are tough issues, but I don't want to allow those emotions to rule my life. I don't want to feel sorry for myself all the time, and I certainly don't want to allow the mistakes of my ex-husband to continue to bring me down!

Even though I was appalled at the idea of being single in my mid-40's, I did start dating about eight months after my ex moved out. I am now in a very nice relationship with a very good man who swears he is NOT gay! I don't know if this is "the one," but I'm enjoying having a man appreciate me as a woman, in all areas of my life. And yes, the sex is MUCH better with a straight man than with a gay man!

I still question my judgment as far as love and relationships in general because of my lousy track record. The first guy I dated after the break-up with my ex ended up stalking me, but I gain a little bit of confidence every day. I am anxious about my future, but honestly, who isn't? Even when I was married, I would worry about how things would be after the kids left for college, about how things would be when we retired, and on and on.

So I try to live one day at a time and to be grateful for the good things in my life. I have found that there IS life after being married to a gay man! It may take awhile to find your way, but you will because you owe it to yourself and your kids, if you have them. Yes, you've been mistreated, but now it's your turn to take control of your life. It will be scary at first, but you'll find a way. And you will have your "up" days and "down" days. But ultimately, you will be better off not living a lie anymore. As they say, the TRUTH always wins out.

PROFILE #8: JANE B., Texas, married 30 years, divorced for two years, one adult daughter, Human Resources professional. My gay spouse never admitted his homosexuality, even when I had mounds of evidence: photos, love letters, and airline tickets. He treated me like the "enemy" during the divorce and made sure I was financially destitute in the end.

I was raised by parents who never touched each other, hugged, or even feigned fondness or compatibility. They voiced an intense disapproval of physical displays of affection, even if engaged by movie or television characters. My mother was extremely critical and negative, as well, of me and my three siblings, so I certainly didn't ever feel like I was special or deserved to be cherished as person. You hear the expression "it was a labor of love." My mother simply acted like it was all labor to do anything for us. She treated us as if we were unwanted, a huge burden, and the cause of her misery. No wonder that I accepted "second class" treatment from my own husband. I accepted, however, he chose to treat me without asking for more, without demanding more, without expecting more. I let him dominate me, much as my mother had dominated me and caused me to doubt myself in every aspect.

I wasn't allowed to date until I left my parents home, away at college. As a result, there was no maternal or adult guidance about what constituted a decent marriage partner. I dated a lot during my freshman year – but never anyone for longer than a few months. I dated my ex exclusively beginning sophomore year, for a total of five years before we married at ages 25. For 30 years, I believed that what I had was as good as it gets. I look back and realize I had no soul during the marriage, no real identity within the marriage (although I was very successful at work) and was depressed much of the time – but I was too scared to let go, too insecure to stand up for myself and ask why our marriage did not make sense – why he was constantly gone, why there was no savings, no money despite high earnings (that I never saw), why he verbally abused me in front of our child.

Not a pretty picture, but that was me, in my marriage. To the outside world, we were the "it" couple – the one everyone wanted to socialize with because we were fun, vibrant, and lively – but when it was just the two of us, there was no intimacy, no relationship, no respect – because he forbid it, and I accepted it as the status quo.

Red Flags – Signs I Missed

I used to think the kinds of things I've listed in the first section were mere stereotypes of gay men – the kind who dresses up in outrageous costumes at Halloween. Although gay men who marry straight women cannot indulge in outward expressions of their homosexuality, they are not exactly like straight men, either, if you look behind the closeted door.

Behind the closeted door, we had a 30 year marriage that he led me to believe was normal – but in hind sight, I know it was empty and loveless on his part and anything but normal. If I ever questioned anything, he asserted that there was something wrong with me, that my expectations as a wife and mother were way out of line. In looking back, I know I missed some all too obvious "clues" that he never loved me in the way that a man and woman are meant to be in love.

I lived in a fog . . . I recall thinking, during most of the marriage, that I lived in a Bizarro World where even the simplest things were difficult and certainly never made sense. Things that should have been easy were never easy with him. He was unhappy, living a tortured double life, and treated me like a roommate at best – someone you live with but do not regard as your cherished wife.

Beyond BARBARA STREISAND and BROADWAY MUSICALS or stereo-typical, near-comical signs, if only he were not my husband.

1. His obsession with Clinque skin care products – it was the men's line of products, not women's, but he did buy A LOT. How much? Enough to alarm store management on several occasions because they thought he was buying for illegal over-seas re-selling. Several stores had him on a list that limited him to a small number of purchases each time.

And I thought he was just ahead-of- his time as a "metro sexual," you know, those cool urban men who take great care of their skin!

2. His collection of Lalique fish – it never occurred to me that straight men don't collect small (about 2 inches high) glass sculptures, each priced at $100. Because this is what he liked, I bought them for him for each special occasion, so he had about $3,000 worth. Baseball cards? Nah! Golf equipment? Nah! Tools? Nah! He wanted little high priced glass fish in a multitude of colors and stored them in a lighted glass curio cabinet from Nieman's!

3. Love of hot baths – he showered on week days, but on weekends... there he was, luxuriating for hours in our Jacuzzi bath tub.

4. Shoe obsession (men's shoes) but he was like Imelda Marcos in the number he had – over 50 pair, all expensive. He also loved designer clothes, especially jackets and coats.

5. Women's jewelry – he bought them for me, but they were always Amazon sized; couldn't even wear some of the pieces he selected because the sheer weight of the necklaces caused me pain. I think now that he was secretly selected jewelry that would look good on his 6 foot frame, not my 5'4" body.

6. Women's fashion – he followed women's style like a fashionista – knew before I did if the fall hemlines were going to be long or short.

7. He did love Barbara Streisand, Bette Midler, musicals, flower arrangements, and China dish patterns... and there were other tell-tale signs:

    a. Disinterest in ALL sports. Okay, maybe there are straight men that don't follow sports, either. But my ex couldn't stand watching or participating in ANY (except liked to watch women's figure skating).

    b. Avid Oprah Book Club fan – he bought them, read them, and then passed them on to me.

    c. Insisted on selecting all of our daughter's clothing from infancy to pre-teen. I wanted her in cute little Oshkosh B'Gosh toddler overalls; he dressed her in extreme children's clothing from New York City that would have been appropriate for a miniature outer space being.

    d. Hated all home repair work (never did any), however minor. If it entailed a screwdriver or a hammer, he was no where in sight. Never spent any time doing yard work. He wouldn't know which end of the rake to hold.

e. Wanted to be a house-husband – stay at home and not work. He decorated our entire house, choosing all furniture, draperies, and wall hues. I didn't like his taste, but that didn't matter; he made unilateral decisions, insisting that his home décor style was superior to mine. I lived in a house that had no evidence of me or my soul because little was of my choosing.

And yes, he was a gourmet cook (his chocolate flourless cake was the first to be devoured at the neighborhood progressive dinners); he even wanted to go to culinary school once and make a living as a chef.

f. But, lest you think he was a great help-mate, he was NOT. He hated house-work, refusing to do laundry, dishes, vacuuming, or anything else that would have alleviated my burden as a wife and mother who worked full time for all 30 years of the marriage.

The Gay Husband as Unhappy Roommate at Best

1. Don't touch me, he pleaded! – The sex was bad – his habit was to humor me once a year on my birthday – and I accepted it. But worse than that, there was nothing else, either. No kisses on the lips, no sweet nothings, no cuddling, no "I love you, honey" – ever. In fact, he didn't even want me touching him on the face or arms. No physical touching or any semblance of ardor – except when he was drunk out of his mind. During his drunken stupors, I was seldom a good recipient of his sudden attention, so we did not connect on a physical level. And he implied this was perfectly normal.

2. **A stranger in the midst** – Over the years, as his unhappiness grew (though he hid it somewhat well), he showed less and less respect, consideration, kindness and cooperation. He was the life of the party outside of the home, but with me, he was a different person. He never wanted to please me, even in the smallest ways – like picking his towels

off the floor, even if I asked.

We would have terrible fights over nothing – like hanging up a string of lights on the patio – he would find fault with the way I was holding the lights and storm off in the middle. We were not a team, not a couple now that I look back. We were two people residing in the same house, living separate lives because he would not let me into his.

There was an emotional distancing, a disengagement on his part that I never understood. He was not invested for the long haul and it became harder for him to even pretend there was a marriage, especially when he became involved in a 4 year affair with his homosexual lover, unbeknownst to me.

3. **The Middle Child – in a marriage** – My gay spouse seldom communicated with me, except if the topic was our one and only daughter. I realize now that he used her as a buffer, to keep from interacting on a meaningful level with me. He refused to be a parent to her, so I was the disciplinarian, the bad parent. He was like the fun, big brother, or the weekend dad in a divorce. He was Daddy Warbucks, giving her everything she wanted, both material and otherwise. If she interrupted, he let her, dropping everything.

In fact, she was the "wife" in our family. Nothing sexual went on – but he treated her like a queen (not a princess like so many dads); she was always right, she was protected, she was his soul mate. He made sure of that from infancy on – excluding me when he could, so he could be the important one in her life. A small but significant sign: he never took photos of me and her. I took lots of her and him – but he didn't care enough to capture my moments with her.

If I tried to correct her, he would mock me, make fun of me – disguised as teasing, but it was disrespectful in nature and undermining in front of her. He made sure she idolized him, but only tolerated me. I felt like a second class citizen, like the 5th wheel, in my own family, in my own home.

4. **Travel, Travel, and more travel** – He was a master at being away from home. He either worked late – rarely home

in the evenings--or, he also took "guy" trips (with his male friends) and father-daughter trips, and we took friends/family trips – always in a group. But we never vacationed, just the two of us. He also had a job that supposedly required travel. Now I know that the majority of his trips were not business related. He simply went on international trips with gay lovers and told me it was a business trip. And I thought he was working to earn money for the family! No, he was living it up, expensing the airline tickets and five star hotels to his own company, so I never saw the bills – or knew about the travels with male lovers until the end.

Even when he wasn't traveling, he had a separate night life. He went to jazz clubs, he said, at 2:00 a.m. I didn't go because I'm a morning person. Now I know they weren't jazz places... he was going to gay bars and having sex, while my physical needs were unmet.

5. Financial – A serious discussion about savings (there were none), budget (non-existent), and future retirement (never happened) could not be had. That's because he knew, in his heart, that he would exit the day our daughter graduated from high school, and so there was no need to plan a financial future together that would never happen.

PROFILE #9: CINDY B., Iowa, married 20 years, divorced almost 4 years, two sons, works for a national publishing company for three and a half years after having spent 20 years at home doing in home childcare and raising my own children.

I was raised the youngest of six kids. I grew up with a Baptist upbringing and my mom taught Sunday school. My ex and I also taught Sunday school to teenagers when we were married so religion has and always will be important to me. My ex joined the Navy when we first got married so I have lived everywhere...including Hawaii and California. My boys are now 23 and 21 years old. While married I worked from home doing in home childcare the entire last half of my marriage. I didn't work out of the home so once I divorced I knew I would have to enter the job market with very little training. It was very scary but I now have an excellent job for a national publishing company that I excel at. This proves you are never too old to move on to something new. There is LIFE after divorce from a gay man and I proved it. I am happier in some ways now than I was when married. I look back on my marriage and see that it wasn't as "fairy tale" as I thought it was.

Red Flags

Looking back were there signs? I had people tell me they thought he was gay after we divorced. I often thought to myself, "Why the hell didn't someone tell me?" But then I wouldn't have believed them and why would I? We had two beautiful, intelligent kids and a wonderful marriage of twenty years. We lived in an upscale neighborhood and had all the right friends. We threw the parties and get togethers that everyone wanted to be invited to. Why on earth would I want to shatter that dream I was living? Besides no one told me because they thought they were wrong since he was married and living a normal life.

As far as signs looking back for me, there were only a few. HE was a virgin when I met him at the age of 19. It just seems in talking to women who married gay husbands that most of them were virgins when they married them. He knew NOTHING about sex; I had to teach him everything. And although we enjoyed a good sex life the whole 20 years there were still other signs relating to sex. He wouldn't perform oral sex on me. He said it was disgusting and he wanted nothing to do with it. We had the straight missionary type with little imaginative changes. He also accused me of being a nymphomaniac and told me my sex drive was not normal and excessive.

I later found out after being with heterosexual men to be all lies. I had a normal sex drive and most men do like giving a woman oral sex. He didn't because what he wanted could

61

only come from a man. He did however seem to enjoy sex when we had it which was a lot in the beginning and dwindled at the end to twice a month or so. It really only slowed down the "last couple of years" which is another reason I think that is when he began to experiment outside the marriage.

Red flags others saw during the marriage were varied. Some thought he was too domesticated beings he liked to cook, clean and do what society deems women's work traditionally. I don't know, I remember him getting his hands dirty many times so I never thought much of it. I just thought I was lucky to have a man who helped out in so many areas.

How I Caught Him

I have been divorced now for almost four years. I found out my husband was gay by accident. I wasn't snooping and I never in a million years suspected. I had the wonderful marriage that everyone wanted and envied.

We had just celebrated our wedding anniversary which was magical from start to finish. Then a week later, we celebrated Christmas which was also wonderful with the family around. It was the day after Christmas and HE was on the computer in the office playing Solitaire as he often did the last couple of years. I went in to talk to him and saw him playing but left to do some laundry. Then I came up to talk to him again, but I noticed his cards were still in the very same placement as before...he wasn't playing. I also caught him switching screens when I came in the room. My first thought after seeing the cards unmoved was that the hidden screen was some big surprise he had for me that he didn't want me to see. Boy, would I be right on that one!

When he went to take a shower, curiosity got the better of me, and I went to look. The screen behind the game was for me, it was a letter he was composing. It told me of how he was GAY and how he wanted to tell me but was unable to. The letter was not finished and its formative stages, but I confronted him immediately. I was in shock, horror and felt as though I had been punched in the gut. My heart fell to my stomach and my life as I knew it came to an abrupt end. I have never felt so many emotions in such a short time span as I had in the time prior and after finding the letter. I went from complete joy and contentment of having it all to feelings of betrayal, the lying and not knowing what was real or if any of it had been.

I think that sent me into a tailspin the worst. I felt as though my entire life had been a "lie" and nothing said or done with me was real, but instead an elaborate acting job on his part. I went into a deep depression complete with planning my own suicide. This was the only thing that brought me peace and pulled from my emptiness. Then the idea of my children having to go through yet another blow--another hell--jarred me back into reality. I began to plan my divorce and to get my ducks in a row so to speak when we went to court. I was going to surprise him by how ready I would be. I was not going to let him destroy the kids or my life and not make him pay.

It was my turn. I dug deep for clues, I started to snoop and look for things that normally I wouldn't have given a second look. I found phone numbers, condoms, rendezvous he made on line, going back almost two years. I copied and put together my case and filed for divorce. I also got a restraining order and told him to leave the house. I couldn't live with a man I no longer knew, or maybe never knew at all.

We went to court and I got child support for my youngest until he turned 18, and I got alimony until I marry or die--and I intend to do neither! I have decided for my own sanity that my life and memories were real up until the last two years. It was at this time that his new job gave him the opportunity to experiment with the gay feelings he must have had a lifetime. I believe you are born this way as no one would choose to be gay and go through the kind of discrimination that can follow.

One thing he never did was blame me for his being gay. He told me right off it was not my fault, which I already knew and would never have taken responsibility for. He said he was like that since childhood, but as he got older (midlife), the feelings became stronger and he had to act on them.

Happily Ever After

There is life after marriage to a gay man. I am happy to say. It isn't easy to make sense of it all, and you don't have to. It is not your fault and not your shame to bear. The only thing you can do is try to rise up and start over. This can be scary if you didn't work and have to find a job for the first time as I did, but it can also be very exciting.

I am with a man now that is younger than me by eight years but that is okay (winks) as I have a lot of catching up to do.

PROFILE #10: SUSAN L., 54, Colorado, married 28 years, divorced 2007, two children, professional. Did I make my husband gay? No. In fact, he's still in denial about his sexuality, despite a long history of same-sex attraction, same-sex pornography, same-sex fill-in-the-blank.

Red Flags – Signs I Missed

I grew up as an only child. My parents divorced when I was young, and my mother never remarried. I believe some amount of emotional incest occurred with her. My father was an alcoholic who finally got into AA when I was in my late teens. So I brought a lot of baggage into the marriage and didn't have a good male role model. I was raised in a conservative Christian church and while I had left the faith as a teen, I returned when I was 19. I became deeply involved with a charismatic non-denominational Christian church where I met my husband.

My husband came from a family where porn was the norm. His father was distant and detached or raging, and his mother was emotionally smothering and inappropriate or raging. He was literally raised to be the bachelor son destined to stay at home with his parents and care for them. He was never given the opportunities his brothers were to learn auto mechanics, play baseball or participate in Boy Scouts. Instead, he learned how to clean the house, garden, and play the piano – all wonderful skills, but not necessarily the primary parts of a man's toolkit.

When I first met him, he had moved away from home and had a series of roommates who quickly moved out. The one who didn't move out quickly got into bed with him one night and initiated sex, which my husband claims he never participated in, although he said he was aroused by it. In hindsight, what heterosexual man would be aroused by another man rubbing up against him, kissing, and groping him? Most straight guys would probably rip the guy's larynx out. My husband ended up going to jail for a night because he went to try to "work things out" with this roommate, got enraged and punched his hand through a plate-glass window.

I also noticed that occasionally he sounded rather effeminate when he talked. I mentioned this to him once, and I believe he intentionally worked on it, because for years, it wasn't an issue – either that, or I simply became used to it.

He was moody and volatile. Once when we were engaged, we got into a slight disagreement, and he stormed out of my apartment, stood on the front lawn and kept screaming "bitch" at me. When I called his dad, in tears, his dad told me, "He gets that way sometimes." My friends told me then to get out of the relationship, but I didn't.

The volatility continued after our wedding. We had another argument and he got a butcher knife out of the kitchen drawer and started screaming about how he was going to kill me, kill himself. I ran out of the house and called some older adult friends who came over and told him to grow up.

Immediately after we married, he told me he was having intrusive thoughts about the ex-roommate's sexual advances. He went to a pastor for counseling only to find this pastor also struggled with same-sex attraction and was told that he should just pray about it and give it to God. The next year, our best man called me to tell me he was gay and was in love with my husband. The year after that, I walked into a bar to meet my husband and a co-worker after work and found the co-worker holding his hand. The co-worker was male. My husband jerked his hand away like he had burned it. I said, "Just what the hell are you doing?" He talked his way out of that one, and I continued to tell myself I was just being stupid and suspicious. But through the years, every once in awhile, I would ask him if he was attracted to men. Of course, he would deny it.

After the internet changed the world, he would be on the computer late at night and very early in the morning, telling me he was checking the bank account or working. Of course, I believed him. I believed him when I found an email account with a slightly homoerotic tinge to the name. I believed him when I Googled that email name and found that he belonged to a Yahoo! adult website that had pictures of hunky muscular men in Speedos. He said he was into bodybuilding--he is--and was simply getting inspired. I believed him after I found a laundry list of unknown numbers on his cell phone, called a couple of them and extremely effeminate-sounding men answered. I railed at him, I pled, I begged, but he always denied it. I believed him for 28 years until one night I had one of those "feelings." I Googled the email name again and found him corresponding with another "bi" married man.

Interestingly, our next-door neighbor, who grew up near San Francisco, told me the first time she met my husband she thought he was gay. Then she met me and thought she'd made a snap judgment. Obviously, her Gaydar works.

Blame Was the Name of His Game

Initially, we had a very robust sexual relationship, but then he would get moody and distant and virtually nothing would arouse him. At the end, we hadn't had sex for nearly two years. THAT was always "my fault" even though I watched my weight and worked out as I still do.

Whenever there was a quarrel or disagreement, I was the one to blame – I always had to come crawling back and make peace *unless* he had been borderline violent. Then he was always remorseful.

The financial problems that plagued us from almost the beginning of the marriage were always my fault. I was dominating, controlling, and made our children afraid of him. Forget the fact that he is a sex addict who was expending his sexual energies elsewhere. Forget the fact that he was having professional pictures taken of himself to post on the gay dating sites where he advertised himself as "bi" or "versatile" and not out, but into the muscle sex scene.

Let's not forget that he came from a family with no financial savvy whatsoever and money had always been a huge bone of contention in our relationship that I was always trying to fix until I gave up!

Yes, in the end I was demanding – demanding that he would tell me the truth about what was wrong. I was controlling – trying to control our household to make it normal. These things were wrong – they are the hallmarks of a codependent, which I have been and am recovering from being. How I made our kids afraid of him? I guess I was the one who made him scream, throw things, punch holes in walls, punch holes in doors, curse, slam out of the house, and disappear for hours, on and on and on. Yet when I finally put my foot down last year and called the police – and got a temporary restraining order – I was a bitch who had "done so much damage."

I must add that I believe my husband has some sort of emotional condition, perhaps a type of bipolar disorder, but he has never been willing to be evaluated or be on medications for long. Only after he was "outted" did he start going to therapy for sex addiction and same-sex attraction – and now he claims that like Ted Haggard, he is 100% cured and 100% heterosexual. Do I believe it? Nope, not for neither Ted nor my husband.

PROFILE #11: BARBARA H., 55, England. Together 11 years, married 3, divorced 4 years. No children from this marriage. Physiotherapist.

Blame Was the Name of His Game

I come from a very loving caring family. My Mum and Dad were together until he died at 50 and my Mum never wanted anyone else, she stayed single until she died at 73. My expectation of a marriage stemmed from them, I thought I would find someone and stay together for ever.

I married first at 17 and by the time I was 19 I was expecting my daughter. In my mind I was set for life until he started drinking and getting us in debt. Things went from bad to worse and after eight years, two children, and debt collectors banging on the door, I left.

Three years later I married husband number two. He was very stable, no drinking, smoking or debts. I felt very safe and sometimes bored, but it was worth it to be safe. I was his "Eliza Doolittle," and after 12 years, I was a very strong woman with a high powered job. But then I found out my husband was having an affair with a much younger woman, I wanted to forgive him and stay together but he left me for her. This second failure and loss made me very vulnerable.

Very quickly along came Peter, younger, good looking, fun and very caring, just what I needed as I was divorcing my husband. He explained that he was bisexual which should have been a red flag straight away, but I needed him so I put it to the back of my mind. He moved into my house as a lodger and as each day went by, we became closer and closer. I knew I was falling in love with him but was worried due to the age gap. Silly me didn't realize I had more to worry about, even when friends warned me. I told him that I wanted him to move out as I couldn't stand the thought of him with someone else and the age gap was too much. He said he loved me too, and the age gap wasn't a problem. That was the start of our life together.

The first few years were great; I had more attention in those years than I had ever had. Meals cooked, baths run, flowers from the garden and lots of cuddles and sex. We did talk about getting married, but having done it twice before I didn't want to make another mistake. After eight years, he kept saying "Surely I have passed the test now. Please marry me."

So we got married and then things slowly changed. Looking back now, I should have said something, and I still can't understand why I didn't. I put the changes down to the fact that we had been together for eight years, but now I know it was more than that.

We started spending less time together. He would want to go out somewhere when he knew I couldn't go, so he would go on his own. That was my fault! He was spending more and more time on the Internet. If I walked in the room, it looked like he was playing a game. I know now it was the Gaydar chat room. When I complained, he said it was because I spent all my time watching programs he didn't want to watch--once again that was my fault! On holidays he would insist that he wanted his space, and he knew I didn't like walking (that was my fault!) so would go for a long afternoon walks on his own. It started out now and again then ended up everyday. Sometimes on holidays he would say he couldn't sleep, so he went for a late night walk on his own. It was my fault being left behind because I wanted to sleep. As for sex, well, that was non existent because if we stayed up late he was too tied. If I said lets go to bed early, it was too early for him. Then he would wait until I was asleep before he came to bed.

Things went from bad to worse. I waited until I thought he was having an affair before I really talked to him. That's when he said he wanted me to let him go away on holiday on his own and stay out now and again with no questions asked. This conversation went on for weeks and weeks as I wouldn't agree. In the end we broke up, and I was told it was my fault because I wouldn't agree to his request, watched too much TV, and kept checking on him.

Four years later, and we are divorced. I am lonely, single and scared of having another relationship. I am friends with Peter and he has had a number of boyfriends. But he still says we could have stayed together if I had let him have the freedom he wanted, so it was my choice and my own fault. He can't see for me the choice he gave me was like jumping off a cliff or being run over by a train!

PROFILE #12: ANNE R., 46, Georgia, divorced seven years, two children, office manager

Red Flags

How do you know? Gut instinct? A nagging feeling? I didn't listen to it for years. How could I? I was happily married (or at least I thought I was) with two beautiful children. I was so busy being a stay-at-home mother because the first three years of my daughter's life was spent in and out of the hospital, a wife, taking care of a big house, entertaining, and all the things that go along with a "normal" hectic life, that I couldn't truly see what was happening with my husband. In John's case, he created a life of "smoke and mirrors." Our life together was an "illusion." Everyone on the outside sees something different… maybe there were signs of femininity or the out-of-town trips with James that tweaked a spark of curiosity in some, but those opinions weren't voiced until the truth was known. And only a select few could know the truth.

John has never "come out of the closet." In fact, John recently got married to a really nice woman who, in my opinion, is a lot like me. When I found out that John was getting married, I confronted him about what he had told his fiancé had happened to our marriage. He said he "told her the truth and that she completely understands that his relationship with James was something in the past and never to be again."

Sex Tells It All

John and I had been friends for a few years before we started dating. We worked at the same accounting firm and I really thought John was a nice man and enjoyed his friendship. I was 27 years old when we met and had never

70

been married, although I had been involved in a few long-term relationships and dated regularly. Our sexual relationship was wonderful in the beginning, full of passion and love. We spent all of our time together and he asked me to marry him a year after we started dating. We had a lavish wedding, attended by over 400 friends and family members.

James was John's best man and James gave a beautiful toast at our wedding reception. It amazes me still to this day how these two men could carry on "normal" lives as if nothing was going on between them.

After the birth of our son, our sex life became less "passionate" and more ritualistic. Our son was the light of our lives and our world became focused on him. After a second difficult pregnancy, our daughter was born. Because of her serious illness and the care and stress of taking care of both children, our sex life became almost obsolete. When we did make love, it was quick. During this time, John and I were making love and he put his finger in his rectum and then orgasmed. I was stunned, but didn't ever say anything. But it bothered me immensely and we never spoke of it.

What man doesn't want oral sex performed on him? The books teach us how to give the "ultimate" pleasure. We "practice" techniques; we do "trial and error." I "attempted" oral sex one time with John early in our relationship. He said it was too "painful" and just wasn't interested. I chalked it up to not "doing it right;" whereas it had never been an issue with other men I had been with.

The evening that I confronted John about his relationship with James, he left for a few hours and then came back to "talk." I was still sitting in the dark looking at those Christmas tree lights and rocking. I was in such a state of shock that I couldn't move or function. He knelt down beside me and asked me if I was okay. I looked at him and said, "Did you perform oral sex on James three nights ago?" He said, "Yes, Anne, I did." And then I asked him: "Did James perform oral sex on you three nights ago?" He said, "Yes, Anne, he did." It was all I needed and wanted to know at that particular moment. The tears fell silently. I remember so strongly the feeling of the tears pouring from my eyes, but no sound was coming from my mouth. Terrific pain that I can still remember to this very day.

Blame Was the Name of His Game

John never blamed me for his relationship with James. He has always taken full responsibility for his actions. In retrospect, I believe that John created situations with me to justify his actions. He became very moody and very compulsive about the little things. I can recall one particular instance where both the children had a stomach virus and I had been up for days. They were both finally asleep in my arms when John walked in, said "hello," then got a bottle of window cleaner and cleaned the TV screen. He was very anal about the house being cleaned to perfection, and I told him he had too many rules, especially with young children. He would get upset if there were fingerprints on the walls or dirt on the carpet. It was hard to keep him satisfied with those kinds of things that to me seemed trivial in the big scheme of things. And I was a clean freak! My sister told me that she thought John kept me so busy with everything else that I couldn't see what was really happening. Again, smoke and mirrors.

How I Caught Him

I waited for him to come home. The children were tucked away at a sleepover with their cousins. The only lights on in the house were those on the Christmas tree. I rocked, and I waited, and I rocked. I knew my marriage was over without even confronting him. The gym bag I had opened the day before to gather dirty laundry contained condoms, g-strings, a disposable camera, women's queen size pantyhose and lubricant. This was the bag he had taken on an overnight sporting event with his best and childhood friend, James. I had been suspicious about his "need" to be with James so often, leaving me home with two small children "reminded" that James was more like the brother John never had. James was married, too, with a family. We celebrated holidays and birthdays together; went on trips together; James was our daughter's godfather. And with the innocent opening of that gym bag, the gnawing feeling and suspicion gave way to truth… these two men were having a homosexual relationship that defied any commitments to their wives, their children, their friends, their families, and their co-workers.

"Of course it isn't true, Anne… I would never do something like that!" I rocked and I rocked. "Anne, please look at me… those g-strings and condoms were from my bachelor party (eight years prior)." After what seemed like hours, John put his hand on my leg and I could feel him trembling. I knew then the truth, and I said, "John, it's okay, it's over, I know." And with tears streaming down his face, his next words were "thank you." "I've wanted to tell you for years."

One thing I knew I had to do immediately was to get tested for HIV/AIDS. It's funny how one goes through something traumatic and you can barely drag your feet, but your brain takes over to handle practical things. John still to this day swears the only man he had been with was James, but how can I believe anything he ever says to me again? And how do I know what lifestyle James was really leading? My doctor was not only our family doctor, but a dear friend. When I went to the office that day, I was still in shock and in great despair. I told him what was going on and he, like the few people I would eventually tell, was stunned. All I kept thinking about were my babies and what would happen if we had HIV. Not only was I in tremendous shock, but I was scared to death. John did tell me that he and James had been having a homosexual relationship for 18 years. My doctor rushed my blood work and contacted me the next day with the results. I did not have HIV/AIDS and I was lucky. Eventually, I had the children tested and they, too, are just fine… that is all that matters.

Happily Ever After – For Real

It has taken me years to rebuild my life after what John did to me and the children. I left my hometown, my family, and my friends, and moved 800 miles away just to get away from him and the pain I felt every time I saw him. I never felt like I had to "get him back." Doing that would only cause great pain for the children, and they were too young to even know what getting married really meant, let alone what getting divorced meant. I had my hands full just trying to help them through the process that Daddy wouldn't be living with us anymore. I eventually did a little "rebound" dating, but that was unproductive. I didn't care what the person really was like deep down inside because I thought that no longer mattered. I couldn't trust anyone. I had to deal with my own sexuality . . . my self-esteem, my ego; my confidence had all been destroyed.

It took me years of rebuilding, therapy, crying, and depression to eventually step out of the hell I was tossed into on that cold, snowy December night. There is life, and there is new love, but it is there to be grasped after we have healed. Because only in healing can we love someone again, completely. To take that risk with eyes wide open. And it is beautiful.

PROFILE #13: VICKI L., 52, British Columbia, married 23 yrs, divorced May 2007, no children. Twenty-one years of trust ended for me on February 25th 2005 when my husband wrote me an email at work to say he was invited for an overnight at a boy's house – not his type but thought he should take advantage of the situation. What did I think? What did I think – what a loaded question! I was devastated, angry, confused, hurt but at the same time I loved this man and wanted him to be happy so I told him that I will support any lifestyle changes he wanted to make as I was his friend as well as a wife. It took me 30 minutes to get this statement out of my mouth because I was crying so hard, while he looked at me with utter confusion. Why? Because he felt that his gay relations with men had no bearing on our marriage because they were purely physical whereas our relationship was emotional. At that moment I became a limbo wife with a husband who had his cake and ate it too. It took me 18 months to realize that I could not live like this and I changed. I became strong, vocal about my needs and began the process of shutting down my dependence and love for this man as a wife. Over two years have passed since that time, we are now divorced, working towards building a friendship based on honesty, he has come out as gay and I have found myself once more.

There are many times that I wish we could have made our marriage work – we had common goals and interests, we complimented each other in all aspects of life, we truly loved and respected each other – still do, there was security in knowing that we were family and would have someone to share our old age with. Fortunately for me, I was strong enough to realize that our dependency on each other was not healthy and both of us deserved a full life without the big pink elephant in the room. At 52 years old – I am afraid of the future, I have a hard time coping with trust issues, I have to work hard at liking myself some days and I must accept the fact that the future does not come with guarantees that there is only one person you can truly depend on and that is yourself. Once you learn that lesson you will find strength to move on in life. The biggest surprise is the more confident and happy you become within the more people will gravitate to you – your relationships with straight men, women friends and yes, even your gay husband become better and more fulfilling.

Blame Was the Name of His Game

In the spring of 2006, I was walking across the kitchen floor and my gay husband snapped at me saying, "Do you have to walk so heavy and make the floor shake every time you come in?" Now I want everyone to know I weigh 100 pounds and do not walk heavy but this was about the time I began to count how many seconds it would take for him to find fault with me whenever I came near him. This comment took less than 10 seconds. This comment was also the one that broke the camel's back so to speak. It was there and then I decided I had had enough of this senseless verbal abuse and that my marriage was over. My husband disclosed to me about his secret encounters with men throughout our whole marriage back in 2005 and I accepted the fact that I was in a less than perfect marriage. But I stayed and lived with this terrible hurt, the hidden anger, the lack of communication, the trust and the fear of ultimately losing this man whom I loved.

What other blames were thrown at me – I was told I was a lousy wife because I worked full time and was occasionally late so I was not there for him 24/7. He worked for himself on his own schedule, which allowed for play time with men on the internet and in person. Whenever we went out shopping, he would become angry with me if I spoke too loud, walked too close to him or smiled at others. I never understood why till recently – he did not want a potential man to know he was with a woman. No matter how hard I worked at cleaning the house or looking after our farm and horses it was never good enough. He would tell anyone who came to visit that I did not know how to work the vacuum or that I did not know where the cleaning supplies were, it embarrassed our friends because they knew how hard I worked and they often looked on in sympathy with me. There would be days that he would lose his temper with me and scream at me for absolutely nothing, going back over things that happened in the distant past but totally irrational and bordering on physically abusive. Again often in front of friends and co-workers, who looked on in horror. Lucky for me, I have learned through the healing process that this anger and hostility he demonstrated was in fact his own inability to communicate with me about his attraction to men and his desire to act upon it. He actually thought I knew about the gay thing and that I was deliberately choosing to push it into the closet forcing him to live a lie. In total contradiction to this is the fact that he wanted to tell me but was terrified of losing me so he felt he was a deviant and disgusting while having these desires for men.

Writing this down give me pause to reflect on how our marriages survive for as long as they do with so much hidden in secret lives, with so much mistrust and lack of communication. I am no longer bitter about the years I feel I lost myself while trying to be the perfect wife to a man who could not be the perfect husband. I am one of the lucky few who finally broke down all the barriers between us and asked why he chose to stay with me but treated me with such hostility and lack of affection. The answers I have shared I believe pertain to most of the husbands portrayed in this book – they are afraid of rejection, they are angry at themselves and lash out at us in ignorance.

Excuses Your Husbands Used Not to Have Sex

Well this is the most sensitive area where I admit I felt that I was to blame. Each day that went by that he refused to touch me, hold me or even show any form of caring began a spiral of self hatred of my physical self, loss of confidence and self esteem. When we first met, youth was on our side, all men generally have a high libido and sex was okay but fairly one sided. I touched him and initiated sex one hundred percent and he went along for my sake. He often told me that because of sexual abuse as a child by his father that he was asexual and could live without. About two years into our relationship, we were being intimate and I was on top of him. He looked up at me and said – "I don't like this and would you please get off me".

So for about 18 years of the 23 years we were together, I was not touched in a sexual manner. I even went so far as to make a deal with him – if he would sleep naked with me I would not ever try to initiate sex - I was so desperate for just the feel of a warm body. I would walk up and try to hug him; he would stand stiff and hang his arms in a limp fashion on me. When I let go of him he would pretend to joke and say yuck you touched me. At night I would try to spoon him and lightly kiss his back – there was no response. Sometimes I would become a little bolder by tickling and running my hand over his body – he would roll onto his stomach so that I could not touch him in a sexual way. Sadder still was my unfilled sexual desires, they began to die and fade away until I stopped thinking about being touched or loved at all.

I had no desire, no fantasies and no idea what it was like to be wanted as a woman. Of course I thought it had to be me, maybe if I was prettier, so I always made sure I looked my very best, I thought if I was skinnier he would look at me so I lost 25 pounds; I changed my hair color my brown to blonde; I went to a tanning saloon for ensure a perfect skin color; I even had my breasts enlarged as I knew he looked at women's breasts. None of that mattered--I did not have a hairy chest, a penis nor a beard so I was totally inadequate as a sexual partner.

We did have the famous second honeymoon after disclosure for a couple of months – it was all I had dreamed of and he actually desired me. I thought – wow we are going to get through this and our marriage is okay. But gradually he began to withdraw on me and one day told me that I was putting too much pressure on him to "perform" and that I was too touchy feely.. So that being the case, I broke down and said he could meet his male friends to have all his needs met but if our marriage was going to be open for him then I required the same freedom. He reluctantly said yes knowing that I was terrified of having another man see me naked and that sex with someone else was almost unthinkable for me.

The most confusing part of this was that in giving him his freedom to be with men, he no longer wanted them, he said that our sexual life could be enough if I allowed him to be the imitator. He tried to be with men and said that all he could think about was how I felt in his arms. The mixed messages were so confusing to me because I so wanted a normal marriage with love and affection but was astute enough to know that his desire for me was one of desperation to keep me from meeting someone else.

Towards the end of our marriage, we both discovered ourselves – for me it was the fact that I was not repulsive and that I was a sexual being who enjoyed being touched, and the touch of a gay man was not enough. For him it was that he loved me truly but he could not guarantee to be monogamous but he was terrified to lose me, so much so that he was willing to compromise his identity to keep me in our marriage.

How I Have Moved On

For 22 years, I gave my husband unconditional love, I asked for nothing in return. In the 23rd year I questioned this devotion and began the process of healing by allowing this love to change from love of a wife to love of a friend. How does one start the process of turning off how you love? By accepting the fact that your husband will not become straight, no matter how hard you try to be perfect. That he will always desire someone else because he cannot help his desires. I realized that he still had the wonderful qualities I fell in love with but he was incapable of loving me the way I deserved to be loved. It was admitting to myself that the marriage had been over for a long time and we would not be together sharing our old age. After his disclosure in February of 2005, I began to keep a very private, detailed journal of my journey of self healing. I set goals for myself, simple and obtainable: to be happy with my physical self, to accept and forgive him, to learn from my mistakes and to meet someone who could love me physically and emotionally in a way I deserved. I began to establish friendships with women, something I lacked throughout our marriage, and in addition I worked on feeling good about myself as well my appearance through proper exercise and eating habits. I researched the internet for resources to guide me through the healing process as therapy for me was not an option. **My journal helped me diminish my love for him.**

My husband found and read my private journals – the things I wrote were often in anger or hurt so I lashed out at him in my writings. That was something I would never do in real life. He had been openly seeing men for about 18 months with my reluctant acceptance – I actually would iron his clothes and wish him a great evening with a big smile on my face. Then he walked out the door and I would fall apart only to pull myself together for his eventual arrival back home. I would shower, do my hair, makeup and dress in something nice each time he went out so I would look my best when he arrived home. I would smile and ask how his date went. I would bake special treats for us to share while we talked about the men in his life. But my true feelings about how I really felt were always stored in my journal so when he read them, I felt such a violation of my privacy. **His lack of respect and consideration for my feelings made my love diminish, his violation of my private thoughts made my love diminish even more.**

When I asked for our marriage to be open, I had no idea what that entailed for either of us. Sure he had been seeing men for our whole marriage so the open concept on his side was a mute point, but for me to meet with someone and start to have a relationship was unthinkable. Financially, we were tied together and neither of us has any family so we had to plan our eventual separation and divorce for months while continuing to live together. I was fed up of living in this no man's land of being a wife without the benefits. I told him that I was tired of feeling inadequate and that his anger was affecting me. So I joined an on-line dating site and met someone who understood my marriage and all the baggage it entailed. I went out about 2 or 3 times a week for dinner, coffee, a movie – not sexual dates but the kind where you talk and get to know the person. I always had a 10:30pm curfew, though not once did my husband have a curfew. About the third week, I came home about 10 minutes late. My husband was a little drunk and angry. He started throwing dishes at me and screamed for hours - called me a lying whore (I had no slept with my friend - our dates were innocent) and it was really bad. It was the first time in our whole marriage where I was afraid of him and he was physically abusive. **This too diminished my love for him**.

To make a long story short - he was very jealous and possessive. I let my friend know that I had to deal with my home life first before going any further and he was okay with that too. That night I sat downstairs too afraid to go to bed. He finally cooled off and we talked for the first time honestly in years. He apologized for lying to me all those years and for treating me so poorly. He told me about every single m2m encounter. He was so ashamed of his gay side and felt like a deviant - that is why he could never touch me. His encounters were pretty tame to what I had imagined. I asked him if he loved me, when he did not answer I asked when he stopped loving me. He totally broke down and cried at that point- he said he must be a real failure for me to think that he did not love me. We held each other and were physically intimate for the first time in 18 years. It was my fantasy. He was frightened that my love was diminishing so he tried to win me back through the one thing he knew I needed – affection and love.

The honeymoon lasted for about 3 months. He is gay and needs m2m contact - sex with me was not the same. He became fixated on my innocent relationship that was on hold. Each night he would grill me about every moment I had spent with this friend – if my story changed one iota then he felt I was hiding a secret sex life. I became so distraught over his constant questioning and attacks that I stopped talking to my friends, stopping using the computer, would not answer the phone; I would not even leave the house so that he would have no reason to distrust me. It was a time of total control and terror for me. Then the emotional toil finally had its way with me. I work with horses, often young and exuberant. I was watering them outside and they spooked. I woke up to find myself on the ground, the hose had run the well dry and I felt a little odd. I brushed the dirt off myself and walked up to the house. I was in complete shock – I did the dishes, cleaned up then thought – my mouth feels a little funny. I went into the bathroom and looked at myself. I was covered in cuts, bruises and my mouth was pooling with blood. I had dirt crusted into my jaw and in my hair. I spit out much of the debris, went upstairs, took off all of my clothes and sat on the bed with blood dripping out of my mouth. I had no idea that I was hurt badly and no idea why I did the things I did after the accident. My husband came home about 2 hours later – I had left a message on the door to come upstairs. He got excited thinking I was waiting for sex – but there I was battered with a broken jaw and fingers. My lower jaw was actually in two separate pieces, one side had completely dropped. I refused to go to the hospital I thought I would be better in the morning. He forced me to go and I ended up in surgery with three plates to hold the pieces together. I forgot to tell them about my broken fingers. While in the hospital he went through all my personal things again – my journals, my purse, my emails, papers from work everything. This accident was my wake up call that I was pushed beyond human endurance and no longer thinking. **My love as a wife died at that point**.

I turned to my straight male friend at this time just for support – we emailed and talked on the phone. He said to take to my time he would wait. I was not looking for a lifetime commitment but a man who would be sensitive to my frightened psyche and damaged self-esteem. My friend is nothing like I had envisioned. He is shy and quiet, understated in a solid way with the ability to make me feel as if I am the only woman in the world for him. My husband was devastated that I turned once again for support from this man because he thought my love for him was unconditional and forever. The ensuing months between our eventual divorce and my announcement were a living hell. He moved out on February 25, 2007 and our divorce became final in June. I had to put down that I was the one whom was unfaithful because my ex would not admit his part in all this. This was very deeming for me but worth it to be free.

I understand now much of what happened between my husband and me. We are starting to try to be friends, he lives close by and we see each other once a week for a date of sorts. We both feel love for the other but there is much trust and hurt to heal still. He sends me pictures of his life as a gay man but I do not share much of my life as a woman in a straight relationship because it still causes him pain. My "special" friend and I have an emotional and physical desire for each other that never existed in my marriage. It is so different and wonderful - I am truly amazed at the depth of passion between us. His smile lights up the room when he sees me, he never lets go of me at night while we sleep, he holds my hand in public with pride, he likes me no matter how I look and we spend hours holding each other on the sofa kissing and talking. Just the other day, I planned and prepared a picnic – but the weather turned nasty. I was so disappointed but Ian went and got a blanket, spread it out on the living room floor and we sat right there for our picnic.

I now know that is possible to love two people so different but so vital and important to me at this point in my life and I am now strong, confident and loving life. I have learned one thing - never think that life cannot change in the blink of an eye cause it can and when you are at your lowest, something fabulous can happen - the future holds so many opportunities but you have to be willing to accept that life also holds no guarantees.

PROFILE #14: CAROL P., South Carolina, married 13 years, divorced nine years, two children, elementary school teacher. I was raised in a small town in South Carolina in a Christian, Southern Baptist home. My parents were model parents - loving, happily married, not overly strict. I was the youngest of three children and had a very happy childhood. I was an average student and relatively popular in high school. I went on to college in another part of South Carolina. That is where I met my future husband. We met when he had just lost his mother to breast cancer at the age of 42. I had just lost my best friend in a car accident. I think we became instant friends and confidants because we had both suffered a terrible loss. However, we did have fun together. He was very popular, good-looking, and so much fun to be around.

Red Flags

Looking back at the signs I missed during my marriage, I realize there were quite a few, but I chose to look the other way. His being gay, however, was not at the forefront of my mind! All of my friends were jealous because he seemed so attentive. Actually, he was just more interested in the "girl talk" than talking sports with guys. He never wanted to watch football on television, or any other sport. I realize this does not make him gay, but putting together all the signs, it is just one.

He would have one very close male friend for a while, and they would spend lots of time together. Then they would part ways and I'd never hear of him again. On one day in particular, my children and I came home from somewhere earlier than expected. My husband was there with a guy I had never seen before, and this guy's car was not parked outside. My husband had driven him here. I thought it was odd, but just put it out of my mind. My husband also picked out almost all the clothes I wore. He had good taste but if I disagreed with him, he would get very angry.

Sex Tells It All

The only time my husband ever wanted sex was when we were trying to have children. Other than that, there was absolutely no interest. He would often "fall asleep," but now I realize it was probably just an act. He used to make me feel like I was sort of trashy because I wanted sex more than he did (which was never) so I started to feel ashamed of myself. After years of trying many ways to get his attention such as getting my hair cut and cleaning the house better hoping maybe that will be the thing that gets him interested again, I realized nothing helped. However, when we would have a big argument, he would be the first to bring up the fact that we never had sex! So somehow I came to believe it was my fault.

My husband and I grew up in Southern Baptist homes in South Carolina. We had been told our whole lives that homosexuality was wrong, so I think he married me because he didn't want to be gay. He hoped that marriage would "cure" him. But then I became the trophy wife, and our children were also trophies. As long as we all looked good, nothing else mattered.

Five years ago, I remarried, and my ex now lives a very gay lifestyle in Atlanta. We do get along better now than we ever did before. Part of it was my acceptance of the fact that none of this was my fault, and that he was gay. I have been a "pain pal" to several women in this situation, and I find that helping others through it helps me at the same time.

❖

PROFILE #15: PATTI T., 50, Missouri, married 24 years, separated two years, divorced one year, one child, administrator.

Red Flags

He was the most intense, driven man I had ever met. In fact I told many people that I was attracted to him because he had set goals; none of the previous men I had dated had seemed to have any sort of life plan they were following. They were content to drive trucks or punch a clock and collect a paycheck. This man was extremely intelligent, vibrant, and charismatic. He was spontaneous; he had a great sense of humor and was so romantic. This man had seemed so different. Little did I know just how different.

He swept me off my feet and we were engaged within just a few months. Because I wanted to spend every moment with him, I willingly let my relationships with friends and family take a back burner. Later, when I started to renew those ties he found ways to keep me from them. He let me know how much he disliked my friends, made excuses to avoid family events, and started arguments to keep me from attending things. Many times it was just easier to go along than to fight.

Isolation seems to have been a large part of his control over me. We constantly moved--27 moves in 24 years. Sometimes just from an apartment to a house, but there was also five out of state moves as well. Each move made making and giving up friends hard. There was no ability to develop deep relationships with other women to compare my life. My son has no idea where home is because it was constantly moving. Every time a move took place we automatically had to cling to each other for support and companionship during the settling in process. I now believe that many of those 'company' mandatory moves weren't for real, and he arranged them so that we would constantly be kept off balance.

He loved to cook, he was a clean freak—not that he cleaned, he just expected me to clean at a certain level of excellence. He didn't like sports; he preferred gardening, and watching birds and other wildlife. He claimed to love fishing, but I can't ever remember him bringing home any fish.

He was an impeccable dresser and loved to imitate whatever was popular from GQ magazines. He refused to shop where we could afford to buy--WalMart--and we would have to charge his clothing at more expensive places. My son says the ties he wore were a dead give-away that he was gay. I always had admired his taste in ties and felt he made very bold statements with color and pattern. Who knew? I've often said, "Show me the book that says, this means a man is gay." But my son just shakes his head and says, "There is no book mom, you just know." How? How does one just know? I certainly didn't know!

He had a strong relationship with his mom; she called him every night at dinnertime. He liked to cook, but lots of men like to cook. He had terrible decorating sense so that wasn't a clue. Lack of sex was the only outward clue that anything was wrong.

Sex Tells it All

Not Tonight Dear... My husband wasn't interested in sex. He seemed completely normal before we married but his interest quickly waned. Each time we separated there was a brief period where he renewed interest but as soon as he had won me back he would loose interest again. I used to say he was a great at the chase but had no follow-through.

Blame Was the Name of the Game

...Uh, must be the cold medicine I took last week!

My husband didn't take responsibility for anything. It seems that no matter what the problem was, it was my fault. Dinner wasn't good enough, hot enough, too hot, child is crying, room too hot, too cold, nothing is clean enough, something smells in the refrigerator, where's my hammer, I know you must have used it... You're too fat, you repulse me, how could you forget to pick up the dry cleaning? Why don't you think, why don't you do something different with your hair, why don't you go blond... etc., etc., etc.

It truly didn't matter what I did or how I did it. I'd changed my hair color and style so many times by the time I'd finally figured out what was going on, that I couldn't remember what my real hair color looked like! Nothing was ever clean enough. Every night when we sat down to dinner, I apologized before anyone took a bite to try to head off any anger and insults— and I am actually an excellent cook!

I was expected to cook, clean, mow, and do laundry, help with all outside work, take care of a child, work outside the home, home school, and entertain. Once I painted the entire outside of our house in the heat of the Texas summer by myself—this after maintaining the above list each week. In the end, he had gotten to the point that he would feel sickly and weak after very short periods of time working outside, and he would have to return to the office. The stress of his job was getting to him you know!

As far as sex goes, he mostly blamed me. I was too fat. But he also mixed in things like stress of job, cold medicine, not feeling well, headache, picking fights, etc. Most of the time, I just avoided bedtime altogether by needing to stay up and do one last load of laundry or some other activity so that he would be asleep when I got to bed.

Once in awhile in his sleep he would reach for me. His hand would be sticky, clammy—kind of like a perverted old man. His hand would be very shaky, and he always reached and groped my rear. If I turned to him and tried to guide his hand anywhere else or tried to wake him for sex, he would pull away and roll over. Many nights I cried myself to sleep.

The Truth Behind His Lies

My husband finally confessed to having gay encounters after our home had been searched by the police on a report that he was downloading child porn. It turns out that not only is he gay, he is a gay pedophile. He later told me the counselor said he wasn't gay or a pedophile, but rather that he was a sex addict! My response was that an addict will use up everything at home then go look for more. Since he never wanted me, I don't believe he was a sex addict. If your husband tells you this think twice. I think this is just a new label to make men look good. It sickens me to think I was married to him for so many years. Thinking of those sticky, clammy, perverted old-man hands groping me turns my stomach, and I always feel the need to go take a shower to cleanse myself again. He now sits in a prison cell.

Happily Ever After – For Real!

I'm still working on the happily ever after part. My son, who is so wonderful, has begun sinking into drugs and just last week, I had to ask him to leave the house. I am so angry because even though these decisions are ultimately my son's, I know it is because of the pain and devastation his father has caused. We have never heard an apology from him. Because he went to prison for the child porn, the court was unable to give me any dollar settlement in the divorce. Therefore I was left with all the bills, the mortgage, and other expenses. I lost the home and the cars. I am still trying to dig myself out of the financial mess I was left with. I will admit I love going home at night. I sleep through the night. I have not once experienced loneliness. I am alone but not lonely. I am learning to love my*self*. I don't know if I will ever trust a man enough to let him close enough to me to have a real relationship. Even after three years, I have no desire to even pursue such a thing. I'm having a great time just discovering who I am, what I really like, and how deep my gifts and talents go. I'm still finding my way in the world and wondering how God is going to use this for His glory. But I do admit…I like my new life very much!

PROFILE #16: VIOLET S. – married 28 years, three children, Executive. I am the youngest of four children born in to an Irish/American extremely Catholic family. I am lucky in that I grew up without dysfunction. My family had its shares of problems and mishaps but my parents were extremely loving and had a zest for life. They passed their love of people and life on to all of their children. I only had two relationships in my life. I dated a boy from my neighborhood beginning in 8th grade. We came from similar backgrounds. His home life was also very stable. We went to different Catholic high schools. I was introduced to my husband by my boyfriend at a high school dance. We started out as friends and during the summer of our junior year in high school I broke up with my first boyfriend and began dating my husband. My husband's family is extremely dysfunctional. My therapist has termed them "socially inappropriate". There was not a lot of love in my husband's family. He was shocked the first time he saw my brother hug and kiss my father. My mother-in-law once said that she only wanted daughters. My husband has told me several times that I taught him what true love is. If that is really true, then how did this happen to me?

Blame Is the Name of His Game

I discovered that my husband was gay four years ago not by signs or suspicion but by his own bad judgment. I truly thought I had a great marriage. I married my high school sweetheart. What secrets could we possibly have from each other? We grew up together. I loved him with all of my heart.

It was the summer of 2003. My daughter called and said dad never came home from work. This had never happened before. She said she was worried. I called his cell – no answer. I called his job. He had left early. I called his cell again. I thought he might have had an accident so I called the State Police. No major accidents or road tie ups. I was told just minor fender benders. I kept praying to God that he was not dead. Little did I know what was in store for me.

I left work and continued to call him with no luck. He finally arrived home at about 7pm. He looked pensive and nervous. "Where were you?" I asked with my children standing close behind me. "I left work at 5 (lie #1) and there was a horrific accident on the road (lie #2) and my cell is not working (lie #3)." I told him I called the State Police and they told me that there were no accidents. He replied that they only govern the highway, and he was on a side road. My children were hugging him and just happy to see him.

Afterwards I was tying my sneaker getting ready for my walk, and as I was leaving I say, "I know you are lying and when I get back you better have your story straight." I came back, and the kids are not home. He was sitting on the edge of our bed. He had tears in his eyes. I knew he was going to tell me he was having an affair. How I wished that was what he finally said.

He told me that he was soliciting a man for oral sex, and it turned out to be an undercover police officer. He was arrested for lewd behavior. This happened right in the town we live in. My emotions were of rage, anger, repulsiveness, and I threw him out. I told my children my husband was called back to work. The lies began.

We went to therapy. He told me he is not gay. The therapist told me he is not gay. I began to feel that I was crazy. He stated in therapy that I never wanted to give him oral sex so he had to get in somewhere. "Why a man?" is my nagging question to him and to the therapist. The therapist tells me maybe he is looking for a father figure since he did not have a good relationship with his father! "No," I say, "he is gay!" He stated in therapy that he had solicited men before--apparently dozens and dozens. He told me he could not be gay because he has no desire to perform sexual acts on a man. He just wanted a blow job that I would not give him.

So now it is my fault. I began to blame and question myself. Maybe he is not gay, he is right I should have performed oral sex. He tells the therapist that I can be prudish. He always wanted to "Kick it up a notch". The blame game continued on and on until finally I left him to his therapist and got my own.

My therapist who I am still with today feels he is bisexual. Bisexual is a highly overrated word. But after a year and a half of a roller coaster of emotions and my self-esteem being in the basement, I finally decided that I have to rise out of the rubble and better myself from this situation. I basically live a life that is a lie right now. I have a husband who four years later still insists that he is not gay. He can convince himself he is not, but he will never convince me.

We are still married although sex between us is not an option. His elderly parents live in our home further complicating things. I think if I was to share with my children or with my in-laws that my husband was a Gay American they would think I was a liar. That is how good he is at keeping his secret.

I do not blame myself for what has happened between us. Our marriage vows were to love and honor. I respected and kept that promise, so I have no blame in any of this. I continue to honor him by not letting his secret be known to his parents and our children.

My children are all college age adults now. Over the past year I have let them know that their father and I have not been getting along and may be heading towards separation, so that when it happens it will not be a shock. My husband will not fight me on any of it. I learned early on to play the game – I kept all of the paperwork related to his arrest and court appearance related to his arrest. I put them in a safe deposit box in an undisclosed bank. I will use them if I have to. I know that when I close this chapter of my life there will be another chapter beginning. I am no longer afraid to face anything as a result of what has happened to me in the past four years.

PROFILE #17: SHELLYE H., 36, Texas, married 13 years, separated 2 years, two children. My husband Dean and I met on September 16, 1986. We married April 9, 1994. Our marriage dissolved February 13, 2005. He moved out February, 2006.Our divorce is due to be final in June or July 2007.

Red Flags – Signs I Missed

Dean and I met when were in high school, 20+ years ago. We were high school sweethearts, both 15 years old when we met.   Dean had many female friends and one very best male friend that "came out of closet" after a failed relationship with a girl in high school. He had no interest in sports of any kind, either playing or watching. He never had an interest in cars, fishing, hunting or doing any guy things. He loves designing flower arrangements and interior design. Dean likes to cook, and he is a clean freak. He is well-groomed – perfect hair, perfect nails, perfect clothes, and has a perfect house. I initially blamed all of these things on the fact that his mother raised him and that seemed to work with me and with my friends. He did have an older brother and a father in the picture but that seemed irrelevant until now.

Sex Tells It All

When I look back, I remember how strange it was that he didn't kiss me until New Years Eve, 1988 (over two years after we met). I remember having to ask for that kiss.

We slept together for the first time in September 1989, a full three years after we met. I look back now and there were so many signs. I was teased in high school about my boyfriend being gay (could they see it?). There was NEVER sex unless he initiated it. He was great at foreplay but was the kind to climb on, do the deed, get up, clean up and turn his back on me. Even on the night of our honeymoon, we didn't make love. When we did make love, it never happened more than once in a week, never more than once a day and never anytime but after dark in the dark and with his eyes closed. I believe he never really wanted to touch me, and I now know he was never turned on by my touching him. He never talked about sex either, never ever.

How I Caught Him

I was very fortunate that I did not catch my husband. Even worse, I didn't even suspect! We had everything – the house, the white picket fence, two kids, one dog, and one cat. I will never forget that day...

February 13, 2005 was the day my life crumbled. That day started out as any other. I came home the previous night day from an out of town trip which lasted nearly a week. I came home not only to spend his weekend off with him but also because it was going to be Valentine's Day. It is not that Valentine's Day was anything really special – no occasion was - but I could still hope this one would be. That afternoon I went shopping as I usually did, came home, and sat down on the couch. I remember he got out a cigarette.

His New Year's Resolution was to quit smoking, and to my knowledge, he had stuck to it. I missed the kids and when I asked where they were, I was told they were with a friend because he needed to talk to me. I asked him what was going on and out of the clear blue he said, "I THINK I AM GAY!" I about choked, burst into tears, and then finally mustered up, "You have to be kidding me! I have to be having a nightmare!" Throughout the next hour or so, I asked small questions. I asked if he thought maybe he was "bi" and his answer was "maybe." He proceeded to tell me he wanted to try and see what it would be like to have a relationship with a man. He told me that he did not want to be single again and that he would either be with me or with a man. He said he would never put my health in jeopardy and that if he was ever with a man, he would tell me. He told me this as if he was telling me he was losing his job or something. I couldn't believe it! All I kept saying was I had to be in a nightmare and I would wake up soon. I even pinched myself over and over.

I did ask my husband THAT BIG QUESTION EVERYONE WANTS TO KNOW. "Why didn't you tell me?" You wouldn't believe his answer – "YOU DIDN'T ASK!" He is right, I didn't but let me tell you -- I will NEVER make that mistake again. It is now the first thing I ask. It comes right after "hello!"· Ask my boyfriend!

The Truth Behind His Lies

I was, before we were married, aware of one encounter involving a gay man, but I was led to believe that that encounter was NON-consensual. I found out only a year or so ago that that encounter was not only one, but two with different men and the NON-consensual part--well, it could have been stopped if he had wanted it to be.

Happily Ever After – For Real!

Like I said, Dean and I are in progress of getting a divorce. He filed in December 2006. It is not what I want, but it is what I need. I love him and that I always will. It is horrible when you are 36 years old and trying to get over your first love. We were best friends in the beginning, and even today, two years after he came out to me, we are still friends, though these days, I think calling us best friends is a little extreme. We share a house together again – he, his partner, our children, his partner's children and me. It sounds strange but it works for now.

As far as my life goes, I have met a really, really nice man that is straight. He enjoys being with me. It is important to him to show me that I turn him on. The best thing about him though is that he can relate to where I have been and where I am going. His ex-wife left him for a woman. He has had several more years of "getting over it" than I have, but he doesn't blame me for my husband and doesn't hold my husband's choice against me. He tells me everyday that he is glad my husband is gay because that allows me to be available for him. I don't know what the future holds for us, but

I do know that I do need him in my life. I am still a woman with the desire and need to be with a man. The fault in my marriage was NONE of my doing.

PROFILE #18: SHIRLEY M. I live on the Far North Coast of Australia, near Byron Bay. I met Don, who comes from London, England seven years ago on a chat site called ICQ, we had chatted everyday and became good friends. I flew to London to meet Don 10 months after we started to chat. On first meeting Don, he seemed such a gentleman. I was swept off my feet. I had originally gone for a three-week holiday, but stayed on for six weeks. We were in LOVE, such the perfect couple. I flew back to Australia, put my affairs in order, and then returned back to London, to live with the love of my life for another six months. Over this period of time, our love had deepened to the point where we could not live without each other. So plans were made for Don to immigrate to Australia, and I was to sponsor Don, with costs of immigration, airfares, and other expenses. Of course there wasn't ever any doubt about the cost, for we had to be together. After all, ours was the perfect match, made in heaven. A dream, a real fairy tale, and meeting the man of my dreams--what a lucky girl I was.

Red Flags - Signs I Missed

Looking back, the signs were there, but I just didn't see hem. When in Vancouver, I had received a phone call very early one morning, from Australia, saying my beloved Grand Mother had passed away. Poor Don, his sleep had been disturbed. He was so comforting towards me when he said, "Why did they call so early in the morning, when she [my grandmother] had been dead for a few hours?" and "They could have waited for a more civil time, and what was the difference as she was already cold and dead." Such comfort during the time, I needed a cuddle, but no, he only abused because my Grand Mother chose to die. No compassion, not a thought of how I felt. I remember looking into his cold, cold blue eyes, and thinking to myself, "What a jerk." That night he came home with a dozen red roses and was ever so sorry. Don was a very cold person--I won't even call him a man. When we went out with his family and friends, he treated me like a princess, held my hand, and was very loving, but behind closed doors, things were different--heartless, cold, at times bitchy. But his promise of "Things will get better, just give it time," kept me hanging in.

Blame Was the Name of His Game

After Don immigrated to Australia, he would just sit around, and expect money to be handed to him. He would sleep all day, and drink all night, but it wasn't his fault that he had to sit around, or sleep all day, it was the Australian Government's fault, as he didn't have work rights. He couldn't do house work because that was my job. Needless to say, I was working full time, 14 hours a day, 5 days a week. It wasn't Don's fault that he had to drink a mickey of Vodka every night, then 12 cans of beer because it was the Australian Governments fault, due to not having work rights. And then it was also my fault that I didn't have the $4,000.00 for immigration to be completed, so Don could get work rights. It wasn't his fault that he was busted for drink driving, with high alcohol content, and that I had to pay $600.00 for a lawyer, to save Don from having a record, which would have gone against him with immigration. It wasn't Don's fault that he couldn't drive on our roads with a high alcohol reading, it was our Police Department's fault, for having such stupid road rules. It wasn't Don's fault, that his car, which I bought him out of money my Grandmother had left me, had been smashed. The whole left side of the little car wiped out the side of the house. Anyhow Don said it was just a piece of junk that little car. It wasn't Don's fault that he was in Australia--he was here just for me, as he LOVED ME. I was a lucky girl. Ah yes, things will get better. Just give it time Shirley.

Sex Tells It All

Yes well, SEX, or should I say LACK of it. Don had this strange fetish, a foot fetish. He would suck my toes and play with himself, and that was our SEX. When he would finish, he would say, "Gee love that was great." Meanwhile I'm waiting for a little bit of love, lying next to him, bright eyes, in lovely nightwear, thinking to myself, when will it get better? Don and I would talk about our joyful sex life, and he would say it great, and I didn't want to hurt his feelings. Don would say, "For God's sake, give it time, it will get better.

Don didn't like to shower very often or change his underwear. His reason was that he suffers from dry skin, and the water from the shower use to hurt him. Oh yes, Don was very good at excuses; he was the master of excuses. This went on for six years. In public, Don would pinch me on the rear, and act like a real macho man, very odd behaviour--so manly to the outside world. He would drown himself in cheap aftershave; after all he couldn't shower. And he couldn't touch me, as he wasn't clean due to his skin condition. If I complained about lack of sex, I was told, GIVE It TIME. After all we LOVED each other, and Don would tell me that God had meant for us to be together. I know I probably sound like a rather silly woman, but I was in love with the man of my dreams. Yes, I knew he had issues with his skin and then there was his bad back, and after all none of this wasn't his fault. HMMMMMM.

How I Caught Him

Late one night I had been in bed asleep, and I needed to go to the bathroom. As I made my way to the bathroom, Don was in his usual place, sitting in the lounge chair, drinking, and he had his laptop sitting on his knees. I had became used to going to bed on my own, as Don liked to drink and talk to his buddies on his laptop. I had never thought anything about this before, as I was pleased that he used to pass out in the chair and leave me alone, as his version of love making was rather repulsive to me. I used to cringe at the thought of him touching my toes, and the smell of his unclean body was becoming too much.

Back to the night I busted him. It was in April 2006. I noticed in the tool bar section of his laptop that there was a flashing orange light. I asked, "Are you talking to someone?" He said yes, just one of his buddies. Don didn't answer the other guy for quite a while. I said to Don that he had better answer the guy. Don was looking very uncomfortable. He told me that I looked tired and needed to go to bed. I said I was fine, and I told Don to answer the guy, as it was rude not to reply, Don typed in "my wife is here" and the guy wrote back "is she nearby." Don typed in "Yes." Don said to me again, "Gee love, you need to go to bed," but I told him that I needed to stay right where I was. The other guy wrote "Does she know what you are doing?" I told Don to move over, and I took his laptop, and I typed in YES! The other guy said "she must trust you" and I typed in, "Yes, she does trust me." The guy thought he was still chatting to Don, but it was me, Shirley, that he was talking to. Don had gone to bed, saying as he was walking away, that he had nothing to hide and I was carrying on like a stupid woman.

Some time later, I bought up the history and my God, what I read. I remember looking at my darling mother's photo. She had passed away, a few months before. I had my hand over my mouth, to stop my screaming. Here it all was--my partner of nearly seven years, who swore love to me till the day we die. He wrote that he was Bi-sexual, and that his wife [me] wasn't to know, and she [me] couldn't know. He wrote about the things he planned to do with the other guy. Don wrote that he loved to suck men's penises. I was so devastated as I knew my mum was watching the pain I was going through. How could I have not seen the signs? But in all honesty, I wasn't looking for things like this. How could I see the signs? My man hated gay men, and he even made fun of them in public. But the proof was in his words that he wrote. Then things started to make sense to me, all the lies, the excuses, the lack of compassion, the coldness, yes and even the bitchy attitude.

The Truth Behind His Lies

After I found the truth, I sat at my computer. It was 2.00 a.m., and I wrote to my dear friend Shelly in England. I told her that I had found something terrible, and that I was unable to tell her what I had found. I didn't sleep at all that night, and I couldn't work the next day. When I confronted Don with what I had read, he said that I was overreacting, and that it was a big joke--he was leading the other guy on. Sure some joke! Don and I stayed together for another six months. During that time I was able to really stand back and have a good look at what I was dealing with. Don kept denying about his sexuality, and he even threatened to leave me if I kept talking about it. He kept saying to forget it and move on, and if we did split up, everyone would laugh at us. Just give it time, and it will get better--ha ha ha. During this time, I really began to hate Don, and felt sickened by him, the smell of him, and the sight of him. The funny thing about all of this is Don always said he hated liars, but HE WAS THE BIGGEST LIAR OF ALL.

Yes, I remember on that night in April, after reading his words of disgust, when I looked at my mum's photo, she could see the pain I was in. She could see my tears, and how my heart was broken. In November 2006, on a Thursday night, I couldn't stand him anymore. I told him he had to leave the house. He was sitting in bed with his laptop and he had his headphones on. He said that I was fat, [sure, I had lost 5 stone in weight], and that I sure picked a lousy time to put him out. He claimed that I was the cause of the break-up, as I wouldn't stop nagging, and he wasn't gay, he just didn't like having sex with women. The morning he was leaving, he was whistling in the kitchen, not a care in the world, acting so cold. I must add, after he left, I had the locks changed within hours. The whistling person who was so cool in my kitchen sure hit rock bottom after he was out in the big world. Within 2 weeks he lost his job and was phoning me for food. Mr. Don wasn't prepared for the big world where he had to take care for himself. Yes, I had to endure the humiliation of an AIDS tests, and thankfully all was clear.

Happily Ever After – For Real!

The day he left, he had only taken two sets of clothes, as he thought I couldn't live without him. He was sure that I would beg him to come back. WRONG... I started to cleanse my home of him, and everything he owned was put in plastic bags. It took me two weeks of solid packing--everything he gave me went out. I cleansed and cleansed, as I felt he had no right to even have a piece of paper left in my home. I then went and bought new bedroom furniture, plus linen, spending $2,000.00 on my bedroom. Everything I bought had to be perfect, and to suit only me, and most of all it all had to be girlie, satin and lace, cream and green. I never cried tears of grief, but rather I cried tears of relief. It was like stepping out of jail, to be free of the unwashed, master of excuses, liar. I did cry for days, but all I could do was sigh. I now have my home back and it's just how I want it. No more beer bottles lying around, no more filthy ashtrays laying around, no more bitch of a man. I now know that Don is GAY, even though he still denies it. I know that my mum and God had plans for me back in April, the night I found the truth. As much as it hurt on that night, I had to suffer pain in order for me to be where I am now. I'm, FREE and I do what I want, when I want. I have a special man in my life, and believe me it's great to be loved by a REAL MAN. The world is my oyster, and I'm planning another trip to see my friends in England.

Now to use Don's famous words, "GIVE IT TIME, IT WILL GET BETTER," well it is getting better everyday for me. I now know I don't need a man to make me happy, I look in the mirror and I just love what I see, a lovely trim little lady, with long flowing red hair, and I do turn many a man's head. In a sense, going through all of this made me a better person, and it was a lesson in life I have learned. I'm now prepared for anything; there is nothing that would ever shock me. Yes, I have hardened and my eyes are wide open, I'm wise to anyone trying to put anything over me. I CANNOT BE FOOLED ANYMORE because I don't place my trust in anyone except myself.

❖

PROFILE #19: L.J. I am a forty-eight year old Australian woman married almost twenty-five years and have been with my husband for twenty-nine years. My husband is and always will be in denial. It wasn't until my children grew up and left home, that I was able to face my own truth. I first suspected my husband was cheating on me three years into the marriage. We had lived together for three years prior to getting married. As I really didn't think my husband was the type of guy to have another woman, I soon let my suspicions go. I am still married and living with my husband but working desperately to end this big fat lie he lives. I don't want to die married to a gay man. I once read a quote that goes something like this... "There is nothing lonelier than being in a room with someone that has ceased to exist." That sums up what my marriage is and has been for a very long time. I have lived a lonely life, void of any feeling, compassion or companionship from my husband. I wish I had listened to my gut and taken notice of all the red flags along the way. I have wasted so many years living his lie.

Red Flags

Looking back I think the very first thing I should have taken notice of was the constant stains of sperm in his underwear. It was there on a regular basis. I first thought he is cheating on me but like I said, I really didn't think he was the sort to have another woman. I knew of some men who had sex with men and were married but it never occurred to me that my husband would be having sex with men. It took something far more concrete for me to come to that realization.

My husband worked for his brother and worked the most ungodly hours for the basic wage. I used to complain but he didn't seem to care. I now know why. My story is not just one of my husband having gay sex alone. My husband has sex with members of his own family. That is why he didn't mind not being paid properly by his brother. I wonder now if they were ever even working extra hours or just having sex the whole time. There were no clues that I could have picked up on at this point, but I should have insisted that he work only eight hours and come home to his family.

The stains in the undies coincided with when my first daughter was about two years old. Than I noticed that we were only having sex about once a month. In hindsight I think he knew I was suspicious so he made sure I fell pregnant again. When my first daughter was three and a half, my second daughter was born. I fell into a very severe case of obsessive compulsive disorder. I knew in my heart and soul that my marriage was in trouble and I wasn't ready for another baby. God blessed me with a good baby, unlike my first who suffered severely with allergies and left me very sleep deprived. If I had not had such a good baby I do not think I would be here typing my story today.

Through all my illness, my husband showed no concern for me or my state of mind at all. In fact as the years wore on, he was the cause of my state of mind being so sad most of the time. I should have noticed his lack of caring and consideration for me. This is not normal in a healthy marriage. In fact he made sure that I was sad and felt useless most of the time, even though I am quite an intelligent woman who is more than able to cope with life and what it throws at me.

The Red Flags I Didn't Know About or See

1. My husband rushed the relationship from the beginning and was very domineering and short tempered

2. My husband worked the most ungodly hours with no extra pay

3. Sex became a monthly thing within three years of marriage and a six monthly thing within thirteen years of marriage

4. My husband had no conscience when it came to him spending money and me having no money (This shows a

lack of any real love or respect) I should have seen this

5. My husband often upset me just on bed time. I now know he did this so I would be too sad to feel like sex so he could try and I would not be in the mood. When in fact he didn't really want to have sex with me but wanted me to think he did

6. My husband would often sit up quite late to watch television when I went to bed (Yet another way to get out of sex) or make sure he went to bed way earlier than me and pretend to snore as soon as he got into bed. He couldn't have sex if he was asleep.

How I Caught Him

My husband had a nephew who at fourteen started coming to stay every school holiday. I didn't really catch on straight away as my niece and nephew spent many holidays at my house. I taught my own girls at home and suffered with thyroid problems, so I always looked forward to the holidays and having a rest. He never asked if it was okay for the nephew to come; he would just show up. I was so tired I really didn't need this. My biggest mistake in all of this mess is not standing up for myself and not speaking my mind sooner. As I have become stronger, I have learned to speak up, and my husband has learned to use his hands to shut me up. I had to go to the police about his violence and since then the physical side of it has stopped. He is still trying to control me with anger.

When the nephew would come to stay, he would follow my husband around the farm like a lost puppy. My girls and I would look at them and think it was funny. The penny still hadn't dropped as to what his relationship with his nephew really was. He would also allow his nephew to be rude to me and be greedy at the dinner table, even if it meant our own girls couldn't have meat on their sandwich because his nephew had eaten it all. I often curse myself for not speaking my mind and not seeing the red flags. They were there in big, bright red capital letters, but I just refused to face my truth.

When the nephew was 17, he came to work on the farm for a while. Once again, I was never asked. I really didn't need this. Then one day we my husband, the girls, and I were supposed to go to town for a sleep over for a distance education event. My husband stalled all day on a job and made sure he had excuses not to come with us.

When I got home the next day, his underwear was literally covered with sperm. We live on an isolated farm so there was absolutely no doubt what had gone on. Finally I had my only concrete bit of proof. I confronted him. This is the time he became extremely verbally abusive and somewhat physically abusive. I now know this was to shut me up. This is the time that he started telling me I was crazy and that my intuition sucked. I now realize that at this point I knew for sure. That was thirteen years ago. It was only last year when I found Bonnie and subsequently the Straight Spouse Network, Wives of Bi-Gay Husbands (a support group) and The Leichardt Women's Health Centre in Sydney, that I was able to face my truth. I have been fighting tooth and nail ever since to reclaim my life. I am not out yet but I am working on it. My self-esteem is or was rock bottom. I have returned to teaching and after only six months have been given almost two terms of full time work. Not bad for a crazy, abnormal woman. It is a very hard battle for me as I have to tread lightly with my husband because of the abuse, but I will end this marriage, and I will have peace again.

PROFILE #20: ROBIN K., California. Before I met my husband I was happy, full of life and energy, had great self esteem and felt like a sexual woman. I knew I could make it on my own without a man if I had too. Now I fear that I could not make it on my own. I am angry a lot, but growing up watching my mother struggle after divorce, I am just afraid to leave. I wish I would have left when I first found out he was gay, instead of doubting myself… hoping I was wrong, trying to catch him in the "act". For some reason I think that if I could just catch him with a man… the real thing… then I could leave.

Red Flags and Catching Him

I was 23. I met him on a blind date. The sex was never great, but he was seven years older than me and took me under his wing. He drove a fancy car, was educated, and we could talk just like friends—which should have been my firs clue.

After we were married for two years--and had not had sex--I knew something was wrong. He kept saying "we just need to work on things." I finally caught him by taping the phone line. The first day he was asking some man "do you host or do I?" I still didn't believe it, so I emailed this person to have them send me a photo. I had somehow hoped that perhaps it was just a deep voice. When the man emailed me back bare-chested with no head shot, I knew.

Has my life changed… yes, but I feel stuck, as I am totally provided for and in a million years could not afford my lifestyle on my salary let alone my house payments. So I stay. I still hope that one day I will have the courage to leave. But I am HIV positive (yes, because of him) and I sometimes just don't know what to do. I feel lost and I know I am living a lie, but I am sometimes too tired to change, to move, to hope. I hope this changes one day.

PROFILE #21: SUE R., 40, Chicago, Married 12 years, divorced eight years, three children, Employment Specialist.

Red Flags

I was raised in a Christian home and was introduced to my future husband through a college group at our church. He had a "best friend" that he didn't waste any time in telling me about.

It was if he wanted to set the ground rules from the beginning that his friend was and is to be included in everything. I thought it was strange, but didn't mind as his "friend" was dating my roommate and we did quite a bit together. The friend and my roommate soon fizzled out and it was just the three of us.

I eventually gave my ultimatum and said if the friend stays around, I go. It seemed as if his family and friends were echoing the same thing to him so he reluctantly let go of the friend, but asked me to do the dirty work of telling the friend. I had always known that I was the stronger more assertive one even before our relationship began. I did not mind telling his friend. We went on to marry and moved to Europe for three years. We faced yet another "friend" issue as well when he began working and getting close with a colleague, but it was less noticeable as we went about our newlywed life and discovered Europe at the same time.

Our first child soon followed, and life as a family was beginning. I didn't have time to notice more. Throughout our whole military life, we moved quite a bit. The need for him to be a part of home-life was crucial. Neither of us had any free-time to be out with friends nor even tend to our own lives. After the children grew up and his military career had ended, he took a position in the private sector. Lo and behold, he met another colleague whom he was drawn to more than any other. He could not separate himself from him at any cost. His need to be so close to a man and yet convince me it was because he was lacking a male friend in his life, should have been my red flag. In looking back, I should have known that was not normal for a seemingly happily married man to want to be around another man more than his own family. Perhaps I was too busy in my early motherhood to notice. I don't know.

Blame Was the Name of His Game and Sex Tells It All

I can recall several times during our marriage that I was the constantly being blamed for pushing him to want to be with all of his "friends." I was overbearing, I was constantly called a cold, harsh woman who never admitted to my part in conflicts. I was driving him away. It was my fault. I was told that I was not making myself endearing to want to be around. That alone was all that he needed to move on to the reason why being affectionate was such a problem for him. I was so controlling and over bearing that I was pretty much a turn off to even have sex with. Unless I changed my tune, I was told that this was how it was going to be.

Then, on that rare occasion sex did occur, it was never done to his liking. He was extremely critical and never happy with anything that I did or tried to do in the bedroom. It got to a point where I was actually nervous to go to bed at the same time for fear of the criticism.

When all was said and done and I couldn't take much more, I had confronted him and asked for a separation. We went through the song and dance of who would leave, and we should think about the kids, and should we do the counseling. After all of that was said it done, I was hit with the ultimate. I was told that while he thought I would move on and find another, he would never ever marry again. I was confused and wondered why this was coming up. How on earth could he want to cover this now? I probed and asked him. He became hostile and said that he is GAY and he will never love women again.

I remember the shock in my head. However, in looking back, I did not feel the shock in my heart. I believe that in some form, I knew in my heart. The thing that made it laughable (and I can only say that now) was that he has always said and continues to say up until this day, that I am responsible for making him Gay.

Happily Ever After

After getting through the many, many hours of trying to work through the heartache that our kids felt, I have found myself in a place where my head and my heart know and believe that this is not my fault. There is not one human being who can make you responsible for their sexual preference. My biggest obstacle has been trying to undo the lie he has told our children that I was the one who wanted out, and if I did not want this divorce, we would be a family happily ever after. I have found a wonderful man who loves me in a way that I was in need of but never knew it.

PROFILE #22: MARY O., Fort Lauderdale, Florida, married five years, divorced six months; medical supervisor.

Red Flags - Signs I Missed

I came from a Baptist background where I was taught that homosexuality was wrong. I dated my husband who was 20 years younger than I for three years before he asked me to marry him. Our sex life was good but not that great. He never refused me sex. The last year of our marriage we moved to an area that was 40% gay. That was the first red flag I missed.

Among the new friends we made, three couples were gay and my husband seemed very comfortable around them. That probably was my second red flag. After living there a year, my husband told me that he was attracted to men and thought he may be gay.

When I asked him what brought this on, he said he had questioned his sexuality even before we met. How wonderful that he would share this with me now at this point. Not only was he guilty of omission, but I really had no clue since he was very loving and showered me with gifts from time to time. Maybe that too was a red flag for feeling guilty on his part. Needless to say, my heart was shattered and all he could say was that he was sorry. He couldn't stay in the marriage and keep his wedding vows.

To this day, he has still not taken any responsibility for what he has done. What is really scary is that I thought I was in a stable marriage with a loving husband and had no clue what he was really thinking. I am now trying to move on with my life.

I see a counselor once a week, and she is teaching me tools to use so that this will not happen again. I accept that this was not my fault and I don't know if I will ever forgive him for lying and allowing me to stay in a marriage that was built on a lie.

I might also add that I was the one who had to initiate the divorce. I would like to say that all women should question their marriage from time to time and not take anything for granted.

❖

PROFILE #23: SUSAN F., 43, Gold River (Sacramento County), California, dysfunctional family, physically and emotionally abusive father, married five years, one son, divorced five years, second marriage seven years, two step children, currently separated and in the midst of a contentious divorce, elementary school teacher

The Truth Behind His Lies

My second husband, Dave, and I met through the dating service Great Expectations. Some of his member profile facts were the following: divorced, two children that live with him 25% of the time, Catholic and "maybe" wish to have children.

He further described himself, "I like to feel that I'm considerate and responsive to women, and have been told that I'm extremely passionate and very romantic. As cliché as it may sound, I am every day becoming more in touch with my feminine side, and I absolutely believe it's one of my strongest assets. I'm not afraid of intimacy or commitment."

On the "What I'm Looking For" section of his profile he wrote, "I'm seeking more balance in my life. I am ready in every way to remarry, and I would like to enter a meaningful relationship that ultimately leads to marriage."

Through the dating service, Dave, selected me, and we soon dated exclusively falling head over heals for one another. During our courtship, I noticed a framed family room picture of Dave river rafting with another man and his children. I inquired about the other man in the photo.

That's when Dave told me all about Gary. Gary was a guy he met at the 24 Hour Fitness gym and they had become close friends. Gary even gave Dave's children presents from time to time. During their friendship, Dave suspected that Gary was gay but never confronted him with his suspicion. Later, Gary shared with Dave that he was gay and interested in having a relationship with Dave. Dave told Gary he was straight and not interested in a relationship but could continue to be his good friend.

Often Gary would try to convince Dave to cross over to the gay side and Dave continued to resist and explain that he was straight. Their friendship came to a crossroad when Gary professed his love for Dave while holding Dave's hand. Gary begged Dave to try the gay lifestyle.

Dave explained to me that he could not handle Gary being in love with him and he broke off the friendship. At the time, he still occasionally ran into Gary at the gym. In fact, one time I worked out with Dave at his gym and was introduced to Gary.

One night when I was spending the night at Dave's place, Gary showed up very late because we'd already gone to sleep. Gary probably saw my car parked out in front. Dave went outside to speak with Gary. When I asked about Gary and his unexpected visit, Dave was very vague, and said Gary was probably jealous of our relationship.

Back then, I thought that Dave was a sensitive man and open to having friendships with anyone. He was not homophobic like some men can be. I believed he was such a sweet and considerate guy.

Fast forward to 2007, and I have very different opinions and beliefs about Dave and his so called "friend" Gary. Through some investigation, I found out that Dave and Gary were very close friends. Dave never told me how they went away together one weekend to play tennis and get spa treatments. Also, Dave joined Great Expectations right after his friendship with Gary ended. I now believe Dave may have been tempted to try the gay lifestyle or did try it and got scared. So scared that he ran away to a dating service and stated in his profile that he was "ready in every way to remarry."

Sex Tells It All

While we were dating, I thought I'd died and gone to heaven one morning when Dave sexually pleased me resulting in seven consecutive orgasms. No man had ever aroused me to that ultimate degree of pleasure. I've never reached that magic number seven again, but our sex life was pretty great during our first year of marriage. I loved it when Dave would wake up in the middle of the night and mount me while I was sleeping. Back then, I was in my mid thirties, the sexual prime of my life, and I was ready to make love with Dave as often as possible.

Then Dave's sex drive tapered off. He started his own company with two other partners and was always busy with work. He worked at an office and then came home and seemingly lived in our home office. Often, he came to bed after I'd fallen asleep. I remember calling him while in his office from the phone intercom. I would seductively invite him to come upstairs for some fun sex and love making. Always, he would decline using work as an excuse. A few times I enticed him to come to bed for a "quickie" and accepted that he could go back to the office after we made love or had sex. I found myself always trying to convince Dave to have sex with me.

Another strategy I used was massage. I would rub his shoulders, neck, and back while he sat in his home office chair in front of the computer. Then I would wrap my arms around him in a loving hug and kiss the back of his neck. I remember numerous times saying, "I miss you.....I miss that physical touch." Dave was usually silent and still. He sometimes claimed he was stressed out with work deadlines or projects. My best comeback that he couldn't always ignore was that "sex was definitely a stress reliever" and I was always willing to help him out.

Twice in counseling, Dave admitted my sex drive was much higher than his. Even after his company was established, Dave continued to come to bed late. He still spent an enormous amount of time in the home office or sometimes watched late night television. I recall many nights waiting up for him in bed. I always slept in the nude. Countless times he would get in bed and I would cuddle up to him and start kissing his neck, cheek, and ear lobe. He would lay there silent like a cold fish. I was devastated by the rejections. Sometimes he would give a lame excuse that he was tired or say nothing at all. I would roll back over to my side of the bed and cry silent tears until I fell asleep.

Not only were we hardly ever having sex, but the entire making love became mechanical. Dave had trouble performing and took little interest in making sure I was satisfied with an orgasm. He consistently could achieve an erection but could not hold it very long. Sometimes, he would ejaculate prematurely which suddenly put an end to our love making. He seemed more interested in cleaning up his semen rather than holding his wife. Over time the premature ejaculation increased and became the norm when we had sex.

When this happened, I was always understanding and never critical toward Dave. Secretly, I was very concerned and shared my sex life routine with my nurse practitioner. She gave me some samples of Viagra.

I became desperate to spice up the bedroom scene. After attending a "Passion Party," I had high hopes that some sex paraphernalia might be the ticket to motivate Dave. I excitedly showed him my new cache of lubricants, gels, and edible lotions. He was mildly interested. We tried the Pure Satisfaction Unisex Enhancement Gel only twice. Apparently, the gel worked out better for me than him.

Our sex life then evolved to once a month if I was lucky. Besides not being interested in sex, Dave withdrew from me in other ways as well. He stopped kissing me after I made him dinner. This was a tradition practiced for many years. He stopped holding my hand when we were out. I often would grab his hand to hold it and he would hold on for only a few minutes and then let go. Also, he stopped sleeping with me and would frequently move into the guest bedroom in the middle of the night or early morning hours. This rejection hurt me each and every time.

After close to seven years of marriage, I realized one day while taking a shower that Dave didn't love me any more. I contemplated taking a bottle of pain killers, leftover from Dave's knee surgery, but instead flushed all the pills down the toilet. Next, I called 911 and hysterically begged for someone to take me away. I stayed at Heritage Oaks, a mental hospital, for two sleepless nights and three long days. I was diagnosed with depression.

Four days later, I cooked Dave a special meal for Valentine's Day. I suggested we go for a romantic weekend getaway. Dave was visibly uncomfortable with the idea and so I courageously asked him if he loved me anymore. He said, "No." I asked if he wasn't attracted to me because I'd put on some weight. He said, "Yes." When I married Dave in 1999, I weighted 108 lbs. At that time, I weighed 125 lbs. By the way, I'm five feet five inches (5'5") tall. I worked out frequently, on average four times a week. Dave was a exercise junky. He worked out every day and sometimes twice a day. His body was always super tan and muscular without one ounce of fat anywhere. Two days later, I came to my senses and stood before Dave stark naked and told him how beautiful I was and that if he had an issue with my weight that was his problem. I told him, "I look pretty damn great for a 42 year old woman!"

A few months earlier, I had changed my birth control to the pill. Dave was supposed to get a vasectomy but then changed his mind. I had some nasty side effects from the pill and stopped taking it after two months. I purchased some condoms. Dave refused to have sex with me because he was paranoid I might get pregnant using a condom. He begrudgingly had sex with me after constant begging and my suggestion that he wear two condoms to guarantee I wouldn't get pregnant.

Dave moved out in March and we dated some. One night we had a nice dinner at one of our favorite restaurants. It was planned that he would spend the night. All day I was excited about reconnecting and making love to my husband. I was still trying to win back his affections and love. I pulled out all the stops and created a romantic setting in our bedroom. It was complete with numerous lit candles, massage oil on hand, and I donned a satin sexy black "Victoria Secret" negligee too. I'll never forget Dave lying on our bed. He was completely uninterested in me and appeared like he was about to fall asleep. Finally, I confronted him saying, "What's wrong with you?! Aren't you excited about having sex?! I've been thinking about it and looking forward to it all day!"

That was the last time Dave ever spent the night in our home. And it was the last time we ever had sex.

How I Caught Him: Adding Up the "Gay" Clues

When our marriage fell apart, I asked Dave if he was having an affair or gay. He answered no to both inquiries. He told me that he "wasn't cut out for marriage." I simply could not comprehend why he didn't love me anymore. I was a fantastic wife and a loving step mother to his children who adored me.

Something did not make sense.

A close friend asked me if I'd ever considered that Dave might be gay. She knew that he never missed going to Catholic Church on Sunday and often went alone to 6:30 a.m. mass when the rest of the household was still sleeping. She pointed out to me that Dave may be struggling with being gay.

Dave's sister asked me if he was gay. She had believed in the past that he was gay and then changed her mind after he married me. Days later, she called Dave and asked him if he was gay. Dave's other sister kept saying our breakup was "all about him and had nothing to do with me."

More and more people told me they had suspected Dave was gay.

Finally, I started to acknowledge the possibility that he could be gay.

I called a past counselor that we had each seen separately and together as a couple. I told her I suspected Dave was gay and asked what she thought of my suspicion. She was speechless and struggled to respond to my inquiry. She informed me that many years ago she had in fact asked Dave if he was gay, but she couldn't share his response with me. I asked our current marriage counselor if she had entertained the idea that Dave might be gay. She had considered it but never addressed it with Dave.

Years before I met Dave, I had a boyfriend named Tom. I broke off the relationship after a year. Tom came out of the closet a year later and embraced being gay. At a mutual friend's wedding reception, Tom, my ex-boyfriend who was now gay, was "hitting on" and openly flirting with my husband Dave. Dave arrived to the reception alone before me and Tom didn't know that he was my new husband. When I got to the reception, the flirtation from Tom stopped abruptly. We all had a good laugh about how my ex/gay boyfriend was after my new husband. Dave commented that for some reason unknown to him, that it was not uncommon for gay men to flirt with him.

Besides Dave's close friendship with Gary, described earlier, he also befriended another gay man when he was separated from his first wife. He met this man named Pete in his office building. They became good friends and Dave and his first wife, Shelley, suspected Pete was gay. Shelley told me that Pete would always glare at her, and she was convinced he was jealous of her.

While on vacation, I caught Dave masturbating with a business magazine in his lap. It was open to a picture of a neatly dressed man.

On another vacation, I purchased some exotic body oil hoping to test it out that night. I massaged his whole body on his separate bed and got absolutely no reaction. It had become customary for him to reserve a room with two queen-sized beds rather that one kind-size bed. He supposedly slept better in his own bed while on vacation.

After Dave moved out, he and his son were out getting a bite to eat. The cashier assumed that Dave and his son were a gay couple and mentioned this casually to them. Dave thought the cashier's assumption was funny and he was not at all offended.

At a friend's home jewelry party, I saw an old acquaintance, Carla. She inquired about Dave and I told her we were separated. She had known Dave long ago an undergrad at Stanford University. They were in the same eating club in the dormitory. She told me, "It was common knowledge that Dave was gay but trying to fight it."

I decided to confront Dave and ask him again if he was gay. We made dinner plans and I carefully planned what I was going to say to him. I wanted him to know that I still loved him and accepted him no matter what his sexuality was. I told him that I had evidence that supported something I suspected might be true about him. I said, "I suspect you are struggling with your sexuality." He didn't deny my suspicion and responded that "sexuality" was a topic he'd recently written down on a list of three items to discuss at his next counseling appointment.

Less than a month later, Dave informed me he wanted to get divorced. Again, I inquired about his sexuality and he said he was still investigating that topic. I asked one more time a few weeks later and again he told me he was discussing his sexuality with his counselor.

I believe Dave is gay. I don't know if he's ever expressed his sexuality with another man. I have a feeling he will stay in the closet and may never accept who he really is. Still to this day, he attends Catholic Church every Sunday.

I do to some degree sympathize with what he's going through but it will never excuse the eight and a half years he robbed of my life. I'm still working on forgiving him for that. It's difficult right now because our divorce has become contentious. It's difficult to fathom what's happened between us.

In February of 2007, I received a Disclosure Letter from Dave's divorce attorney. Section 10 describes my step daughter's student loans. "During the marriage, Susan and Dave agreed that they would cooperate with Reagan in obtaining student loans for her. Reagan obtained the loans. It was also **agreed** between Susan and Dave that they would be responsible for the repayment of the loans." All I can think about is May 1, 1999, when Dave **"agreed"** to be my husband and love me till death due us part.

PROFILE #24: LINDA C., 50, Connecticut, Married 26 years, Divorced two years, three daughters, Child Development Specialist. I was the middle child of five children. I had two older sisters, one younger sister and a baby brother. I moved around New England every two years while growing up and we finally settled in Connecticut. My mother was an alcoholic, in recovery over twenty years today, and dad was a workaholic and managed to keep things afloat. I dated a few boys during middle and high school but they were always short lived. My ex husband was able to understand what was going on in my house because his father was an alcoholic, that helped me in making my decision to stick with him. At a young age I was out making money by mowing lawns and baby sitting so I really didn't leave myself much time to date. I met my ex husband at work so we had a common interest, talk about work. My ex was a workaholic and that was what I was used to with my own father. All similarities ended there, with the exception of being able to be a good provider. His parents divorced when he was twelve years old, so we had along engagement because he wanted to be sure that it wouldn't happen to us. Remember the old saying "if you put a nickel in the jar for every time you have sex before you are married, you will be a rich man," that became the story of my life.

Red Flags

In our home, he was the one who did all of the decorating and never let me decide on what I might like for furniture or wall hangings. He chose all of the paint or wallpaper and rugs beneath our feet. I could clean the house all day long and he would come home and clean it the way he wanted it to be. A neighbor at our first apartment complex shared with me that she was afraid that he would wear out the rugs because he vacuumed so much.

When I was expecting our first child, he worked a lot of overnights or late nights. I had fears that he may be out with another woman. As time passed I convinced myself that he was just young and ambitious. That comforted me because I felt so alone most of the time. When our first daughter was born he was the one who got up with her night after night and used to comment about how she would try to nurse off of him, which seemed to thrill him.

At one point, somewhere between the first and second pregnancy, I opened the closet door in the bedroom and there was a picture of a tall, dark, and handsome man. I somehow gathered the courage and asked him who this was a picture of and whether he was gay. He responded with a lot of anger and then I was punished with the silent treatment for a long time. In time we were talking to one another again, however things just never seemed to be the same after that.

I was soon pregnant with our second daughter. It was one of the loneliest times of my life, ignored, how could you do this when we can't afford the first one and on and on. When she was born he did not go near her for at least a month, which drew the two of us closer together, she was my world. Time went on and the relationship was strained, which happens to most when the children start coming. He got very busy with his job and his hobby of gardening, and I got busy with my job to find a sense of belonging. We were civil to each other for the sake of the kids.

Hormonal health problems started to plague me because I was so stressed out. He came to the doctor's office with me and we were told that we couldn't have any more children unless I took medicine to make it happen. We both agreed that we were happy with our two healthy daughters that we had and decided against medication. A few months later when I went for my annual exam, low and behold, I was pregnant again. I drove to his office and announced the news, and I will never forget how he turned as white as his perfectly starched shirt. During the pregnancy, he went and got a vasectomy without my consent. This made me feel very unwanted, and I felt that it gave him a license to go and get that other woman without risk.

As a young teen, our oldest daughter was raped. I was devastated and wanted to take all of her pain away for her. He refused to take her to the hospital and sat silently in the corner. For months it was hard for me to function, so I picked up drugs to numb the pain. We went for family therapy and it was suggested that we get marriage counseling. At the second session the therapist was fired by my spouse, who told the therapist that he would be the one to break us up and not him. All of this time I was hiding my little secret, perfectly functional for work and college and not functioning well at home. Finally my counselor put me into an outpatient program after my two year run. This shows me how much either he didn't notice or maybe just didn't care. He went to a self help group for children of alcoholics and soon invited his two new friends to our home. It was blatantly obvious that they were gay. I justified them maybe being straight, they were from Wisconsin and maybe guys from Wisconsin are different than guys from Connecticut. He began to spend more and more time with both of them such as days at the beach or overnight camping trips. Sometimes I was invited or one of the kids were and other times not. When I finally told him how I felt about them there were only the occasional cards in the mail or the concerts that they attended together.

A lot of clues were there, but I was blinded by love and the whirlwind of children's activities. I never could measure up to his expectations for me, although I did exhaust myself trying. In hindsight, he did me a favor when he finally chose to leave, and for that I am grateful.

Blame Was the Name of His Game

I was blamed for many things over the course of the marriage. Ironing shirts was one of the hardest and most memorable tasks that I had attempted to do. Early on I was put down and told how stupid I was because when one irons a shirt you must always start with the sleeves! Next it was on to the chore of doing laundry, unknown territory for me when you live with such a perfectionist. Funny that sometimes today I still can hear those awful words when I iron or do the laundry.

When I became pregnant for our first daughter it was don't gain weight, I want my wife to look good. He had nothing to do with my numerous doctor visits and was upset that I was going to deliver her naturally. I dragged him to the classes so that he could help me give birth. When the time came he was in the bathroom dry heaving and paralyzed with fear. The doctor told him that it would be a while so he went to the cafeteria and almost missed the birth. I stayed in the hospital for three days by myself while he threw himself into his work. If I hadn't gotten pregnant, he wouldn't have had to work so much.

I took a short maternity leave and went back to work. He stayed home in the evening to watch the baby. He cleaned the house while I was at work even though I had already done it in the morning. I was told that if I knew how to clean right he wouldn't have to redo it. A few years later it was discovered that he suffered from Obsessive Compulsive Disorder; still I somehow thought it was my fault.

For a long time I feared losing him. I thought that if I did things better, like cooking, cleaning and laundry he wouldn't be so angry all of the time. All that I wanted was a family that cared about one another. In the bedroom if he couldn't maintain an erection. It was put onto me because I was too fat, oversexed, or was a mom. If I said anything during sex, I was told to be quiet. He was quite selfish and only wanted his needs met, often I would cry after having sex with him. My self esteem was pretty low and he knew just how to make it lower. If we weren't getting along he would withhold sex from me and with his selfishness would masturbate. The excuse was always that it would take him a couple of days to be able to have sex again after he had it. I was very patient with him but lost me in the process.

If we were invited out by his co-workers, he would always make excuses as to why I could not join them. Usually it was really because we weren't speaking to one another. When it was a function that you really had to bring your spouse to in order to save face, I was taken down off of the shelf and dusted off and told how to dress as to not embarrass him. At many functions that I took him to with me, he would sit there and make jokes about me to make himself look better.

Today I clearly see that I had nothing to do with why my ex husband is gay. He believed at first that he could have the best of his two worlds by stating that he was "Bi;" that way there he wouldn't have had to feel so guilty. Today I have a lot of compassion for the man that he is with because I know what he is going through. No one will ever be good enough, smart enough, or please him enough. Hindsight is 50-50.

Excuses

He could have written the book on excuses to not have sex. Sometimes it was that he had a headache, which I thought was only a line a woman could use. Other times it was because he couldn't function because of his demanding job or worrying about how the bills would get paid. I was told that women don't need to have sex as often as I seemed to need or want it. At one point I was convinced that I was the only woman in the world who wanted sex. When the children were born it was like a vacation for him because the doctor said that we had to wait six weeks. It was okay though if he enjoyed the pleasure of oral sex while I suffered.

Once he was put on antidepressants to help him with Obsessive Compulsive Disorder; he had many problems getting and maintaining an erection. This was a new license for him to not have to have sex with me. As all of this was going on I stood by his side and tried to not seem as frustrated as I was. I practically raped him to have our third daughter. I sometimes today don't feel as though I will ever be forgiven for that one.

When we went away for anniversaries our children were brought along; this way he wouldn't have to have any sex. As they grew up and didn't go on vacations with us anymore, he brought his mother. How many people have sex when their mother in law is in the same room?

When he quit smoking, I became the ashtray of the world. I would shower before bed, get rid of all traces of smoke, and I still couldn't have sex because I smoked. If it weren't smoking, I'm sure it would have been something else.

If I didn't initiate something there wasn't anything happening. Then I was made to feel "cheap" because I wanted sex with my husband. I knew how to turn him on no matter how "gay" he was, and I guess this weak spot in him drove him away more. Looking back, it explains why I spent most of my life frustrated in the bedroom.

How I Caught Him

I was blind to the fact that anything was amiss with him. We both had jobs that required us to be apart, working different shifts, and my working three jobs.

Two of my daughters came to me and told me that their father was acting strange. That meant to me that I had to do some investigating. He kept his cell phone on him or very close to him so I knew that I wouldn't be probing there. When I came home in the middle of the night I would see that he was on the computer and decided to investigate it further. I started by looking up histories and found a dating service. When looking further into it I found that it was a gay dating service. He was up all night talking to men on line as I was out working.

Still I was blinded that there could be anything to this.

Next he told me that he had to work late on a Friday night, which soon became a pattern. Once again I went to the computer and found his profile along with the men who answered his ads. He was e mailing them and setting up lunch dates. I was frozen in fear and wondering what I should do. At that point I chose to do nothing.

My daughters were still complaining to me, so I set up a time to meet with him in order to talk. On that night, we drove out to the shore and he admitted to me that he was gay and had fallen in love with a man. I was totally devastated and wanted to die, this was the truth hitting me in my face. Revenge would be sweet, so I thought. He immediately found a mediator and wanted a friendly divorce, when it all became one sided, his side, I quit the mediation. Soon I was served with divorce papers even though I wanted to try and work things out. This was the end of the beginning.

What I Learned

At first he swore that he had never cheated on me and that this new lifestyle was all new to him. During the divorce, my lawyer asked me to find out as much information as I could. I probed further into his e-mails and found letters that he had written about his "real" life. He had started his journey at the age of sixteen, just before he had started to date me. Blinded by love, I didn't see how gay his best friend, our best man in our wedding, was. In looking through receipts for my lawyer, I found slips from porn stores for the purchase of gay porn films and toys. There were also all of the restaurant checks with double drinks on them and hotel receipts to follow.

My youngest daughter goes on overnight visits and informed me that his partner is HIV positive. When she shared pictures of his family with me, I asked why he was the only brother with straight hair. She informed me that this is the way that it grew back once he recovered from the cancer that he had due to his disease.

When I informed my OBGYN of what had happened to me he started tests for every disease known to man. I can remember many nights sitting up awake waiting for my fate and crying when the kids were not around. I lost my job and insurance and was not able to be tested after the first time, which caused a lot of stress in my life. Today I am back on track and regularly being tested again. My advice to all women is you never know who you are sleeping with so be very careful out there.

Moving On

There has been a lot of healing for me by helping other woman who have been in this same situation or just finding out. I keep myself busy with work and raising our youngest daughter. Recently I celebrated 11 years in Narcotics Anonymous, which helped me tremendously to get through this period in my life. I am careful to not find a man for the sake of having a man because I never want to lose myself again. Some shy away when they find out the reason for my divorce, and that's okay because maybe they are the ones in doubt themselves. At first I truly believed that I couldn't move on without this man in my life. Today I know that this is not true. My daughter and I live in a small one bedroom apartment and the bills get paid every month. We are rich in many ways even though it is not in money. She and my other two daughters can come to me and know that I will be there for them at all times.

People come up to me and let me know how much they admire me for being tough and getting through the storm of my nightmare, and this reinforces that I am truly making it. One day I hope to be able to put a better roof over our heads and we live with the thought that this is not forever. When my daughter has difficulties with her father's wanting to throw her into the gay world to experience it all, she knows that I will lend an ear and no advice. I am the proud mother of three beautiful daughters that are making the best of their lives in spite of it all. One will marry her best friend next month and another the following September and the youngest will pursue her dreams in college.

PROFILE #25: SHANNON T., 32, Washington, married almost eight years, divorced two and a half years, three children, and returning full-time college student.

I grew up in a dysfunctional family, but didn't we all? I am the oldest of three girls. My mom was a stay at home mom while my dad worked. We lived in a small town for the first three years of my life, and then moved to a city. My dad was an alcoholic who would abuse my mother when he was drinking. I remember countless occasions where my father would hit my mom and I would have to gather my younger sisters and run down the street to my best friends house until it was safe to come back home. My mom would yell to me, Shannon go to Angie's house, and we could be there anywhere from half an hour to half a day. It would depend on what the fight was about and how long it took for my mom to gain her composure well enough to stop crying in front of us. I don't really have any good memories of my dad before I was in the third grade. I do remember one day while I stepped in the doorway to my parents room and told my dad to leave mom alone and he flung me into the frame of the door like I was a rag doll. I hit it so hard and then fell to the ground. I could not believe he did that to me. My dad left my mom for two years because he was caught cheating on my mom. When they were separated, I had a very hard time dealing with it. My dad told me he never really loved my mom. I remember asking him why he married her if he never loved her. The words he replied with have left deep scars embedded in my soul and my heart that have shaped the way I look at relationships and how my insecurities have developed. He told me that the only reason he married my mom was because she was pregnant with me. I was only eight years old and he felt the need to destroy me with those shattering words. So at the age of eight, I felt responsible for the pain and heartache of my mother and my two sisters. I felt like all of this was my fault and that I ruined so many people's lives.

As I grew older, into an adult, my dad has repeated the same words to me. My parents tried to make a go of their marriage again, but they ended up divorced after I graduated high school, and yes it was due to his infidelity again. The last time I spoke to my dad, which was three years ago, he still stands firm that I was an accident and that is why he married my mom. He claims to do the noble thing by marrying her, but he has no idea the damage he has done to me. Those words made me afraid to find a man and let him get close to me. I did not want someone to walk out on me. I know the pain I felt as a child from a broken home, I did not want my children to feel that, and I knew that the pain my mom felt was far worse than what we kids were feeling.

I was a good student and tried not to get into trouble. I was not very popular, but I was not a nerd either. I was one of the in the middle kids...in a class of 350, I was just there. I was very athletic and played competitive softball throughout high school. I did not have a lot of friends, but the friends I did have I was very close to. I was considered one of the guys at school. I was the girls that guys could talk to about other girls, but they did not want to date me. I think part was because I was a late bloomer; I was not very well developed until I was almost 20, I was very conservative and shy, and I think I was probably a prude. But I guess being prude didn't really matter because I was never really put into that situation.

I am a people pleaser. I hate conflict so much. I try to make sure everyone is happy and then worry about myself last. I would rather see everyone smile than put myself first. Even though I put others first, I have standards for myself. I will not be in a relationship where I am abused. I guess to an extent I was controlled in my marriage, but it was not something that I saw until later near the end. I wanted better than my mom. She was a great mom, but she only had a high school diploma, and so she struggled when my dad left us. We would have no food in the cupboard so she would sometimes convince us that we had a sandwich for dinner when in fact we had not eaten anything except for the free lunch we ate at school. I made myself a promise to learn from her misfortune. She gave me the drive to get a college education and to do better. I got a two year accounting degree and used that for a while. I really wanted to be a teacher, but did the accounting because that is what my dad wanted me to do.

Sex Tells It All

I never really dated anyone in high school. My ex- gay husband was the only man I ever seriously dated. We dated off and on beginning in the eighth grade. I thought he was cute, but looking back, we were both scary looking. He seemed to respect the fact that I was taking things slow, and I thought he was an amazing guy because he was not pressuring me into having sex. I did have a medical condition that did not allow me to have sex until surgery was performed. I had a septum in my vagina that prevented me from having any type of intercourse. My ex was very understanding and did not let that stand in the way of our relationship. After graduation I had it removed and after I healed he was the person that I lost my virginity to.

We had broken up a few times, and I had the opportunity to have sex with a few other guys, but the morals and values I hold for myself would not let me do that. I have never been a person who could just sleep with someone just for the sake of having sex. I guess I was afraid that what if I got pregnant and I never wanted a child to feel the way I did as a child. I also wanted someone to like me for who I was, and I did not want to sleep with a lot of guys. It just wasn't in my personality to do that.

When you are looking for your future spouse, you are looking for a man who meets your needs in so many different ways. One of those ways is our sex life. No, sex is not the only part of a relationship, and a relationship should not be based on sex, but it is a big part of it. If you are not sexually satisfied, you will be unhappy and that will begin to affect other parts of your relationship over time. That is how things were for me.

In the beginning, we had a very healthy sex life. Not very risky or wild, but we had sex quite a lot. We had our first child when I was 21 and he was 22. Our sex life would go back and forth. It would be on for a while, and then off. Most of the time I was the one who had to initiate everything. I thought that everything was normal, and that maybe he liked me initiating it. One thing that was lacking was that I would perform oral sex on him, but he would never perform it on me. This made me feel very hurt because around some of our couple friends he would always make comments how he would just love to do that to me. Finally one day I told him that if he wanted to talk about and make me think that he was going to try it, that he better do it or else quit making those comments. After that, he never mentioned performing oral sex on me again.

Four years later we had our second child, which was planned, and that is when our sex life almost died. It seemed as though we never had sex. I started marking little dots on the calendar of how often we would have sex. At the age of 25, we were having sex once every three to four weeks. This did not seem normal to me at all. He always made up excuses, and they were ridiculous excuses: I am in the middle of this show (as if the VCR couldn't record the rest for him), I am tired, I have a headache, I feel like I am going to have diarrhea, aren't you going to start your period soon, and I am sure that he had others. I had to initiate the sex too, and he made me work for it. It was like a game for him, he would ignore me as long as he could until he finally got an erection and did not want to get blue balls.

Two years later we had a surprise third child. I love that little one to pieces, and I think he was partially glad because I was not allowed to have sex during my pregnancy so he was off the hook for about nine months; when you consider the pregnancy and the healing from the c-section. After having the baby I did not think our sex life could get any worse but it did. It dropped down to once every 4 to 6 weeks, and it wasn't even quality sex. I saw an Oprah show, and our sex life was in the category of people who were in their 60's-70's. I told him this and he laughed and said that we were busy and that I should not worry and put so much emphasis on sex. He said that we were doing it more than we really were. My ex knew how to make me orgasm, and if I was getting close, he would change his rhythm or finish quickly so I did not have one. As soon as he was done, there was no cuddling or even an 'I love you'… nothing. He would get up, get dressed and then leave.

It even got to the point that he would not do any other position than doggy style. I think it was so that it was easier for him to imagine I was a man, and that way he did not have to see my face, I because just a random act of sex for him. I would feel so used and cheap afterwards, that I don't know why I even tried.

Not only was our sex almost non-existent, but our intimacy came to a halt too. He would not kiss me any more. I might get a quick peck here and there, but no kiss. He never held me anymore. When we slept, he slept on his side of the bed and would wrap himself up in his covers so that there was a protective layer between the two of us. How degrading to know that your husband does not want to feel the slightest touch from you through out the night. He stopped the little hugs and he quit hold my hand. Every part of physical touch was lost as well as my self esteem and self worth. I felt ugly and extremely unwanted.

My ex-husband was my first sexual partner. I think that if I had been with a straight man before, I would have seen the red flag earlier on. Most straight guys rarely turn down the opportunity to have sex. I have talked to a lot of male friends after this and they have said that they are never too tired to have sex. They would like to have sex as much as they can, and if a woman initiates it, wow even better. But they also said that they try to initiate it a lot.

What I have learned from this is that if your sex life drops there is something wrong. Even straight men that are having an affair will still have sex with their wives. It might not be the loving sex that they once had, but they will still be interested in sex. Gay men get to the point that the thought of being in bed with us disgusts them and they can no longer fake enjoying it so it is better to not have it at all.

Happily Ever After

Before my divorce I decided I wanted to go back to school to follow my dreams of becoming a high school science teacher. I had started back to get some general classes out of the way when my husband left me. I was discouraged, an emotional wreck, and financially strapped. I did not have the time for school because I had to work more hours just to get by. My ex had just completed his Masters and was doing great. But here I was, looking at my dream which was so close, and having it go down the toilet yet again. I took a quarter off of school because I could not focus, but then I got my student loans and grants figured out. I filed for divorce and got a set amount for child support; then I set up a budget and ran the numbers.

I found that I could make it work if I busted my but I knew that it would take away some of the time that I would be spending with my kids, but it was something I had to do. I watched my dad control the destiny of my mom and I was not going to let my ex get his Masters and then have the power knowing he kept me from achieving my goals. So I am proud to say that two years later I am still in school, I still have my home and my kids and I am doing it. I am down to six quarters from getting a double degree. I will have my Bachelor's of Science in Biology and my Bachelor of Arts in Education in Biology. It has been a struggle, but I am doing it. My kids see me, and they are so proud. They love it when I share the information that I learn in my classes. The greatest thing of all is that I can show them that they can do what they want if they put their mind to it. The struggle makes it all worth while. My ex is no longer in control of my future, I am.

I have found someone else, but things are different. I love him, and I want to be with him. I don't need him to be happy, and I am not dependant on him to survive. That was the trap that I fell into before. I don't know if it was because he was my first love or if I followed in the pattern of my mother. Everything happens for a reason. I don't know the reason my childhood or my marriage was the way it was, but I have looked back and taken what I have learned and I use it to change the way I live. I still have insecurities, but I hide them better, and I do keep myself guarded to some degree, but I am not afraid to be my own person. I have a voice and I share it, I don't let my new man take control of me like a puppet. He likes that I have a voice, that I share, and he wants me to reach my goals. He encourages me when I get frustrated and he believes in me. He is there to walk the journey with me, not for me.

❖

PROFILE #26: JUDY G., I come from Ontario, Canada. I was married for 21 years and have been separated for two years now. I have three children--one son, 21, one daughter, 16, and a special needs daughter who is 13. I work with developmentally disabled adults in a group home setting, adults with serious life-altering brain injuries in a group home setting, as well as for the school board as an educational assistant to teachers and special needs students in the elementary grades.

I come from a very functional and affectionate Catholic family and had an extremely happy childhood. My ex comes from a cold dysfunctional family. I thought he was perhaps emotionally damaged by this and all I had to do was love him big time. I'm particularly honest, trusting and naive by nature so I am told. I had limited dating experience--only three lovers--when I was between the ages of 17 and 19. I met my ex when I was 19 ½.

I was into my teenage rebellion stage when I met my ex-- rallying against my parents who were too strict for my liking. My parents were disappointed and felt threatened that I was dating "an older man". As in "What 25 year old MAN would be interested in dating a 19-year-old GIRL?" They did not get to meet him for a long time as my ex avoided girl's parents for the most part. In the end my parents came around and accepted him as a son.

Signs I Missed

My ex-husband appeared placid, stable, and mature to me. I was 19 and he was 25. He was different than the boys my age that I'd dated. He was "mysterious"--you couldn't get a fix on who he was or what he was thinking. In hindsight, mysterious was more like secretive. I thought the franticness of horny teen boys was because of fear of getting caught and because they were new at it. My ex was calm. I figured I was dating a MAN now. I called it experienced then. I see it much differently now. Call it lack of passion or enthusiasm.

When we first started living together, I was a regular subscriber to Cosmopolitan Magazine. This was in the early 1980's. One cover story was "Can your boyfriend be Gay? Of all the magazines I've purchased, of all the catchy cover stories, this is the only one I recall him asking me about. My ex asked me "Do you think I'm gay?" I said no , but that he did have some of the characteristics: distant father, interest in art, vanity, unusual walk (yet all the boyfriends I'd had thus far had unusual walks--only theirs was more like a swagger).

Over the years I came to realize that he frequently asked my opinion about gay issues. He knew what public washrooms had been raided before it hit the papers--saying people at work were talking about it or that he saw it on the computer at work... can it be cured... learned behavior or not... locations of remaining bathhouse in Hamilton... In hindsight he had "inside knowledge" that at the time I thought was merely intelligence or a reflection of someone like himself who reads a lot. When AIDS hit the scene in the early 80's he predicted that gays will hide in marriages until this settles... "It's terrible that they'd risk their wives/partners," he said. Intelligent foresight he had.

My ex grew up in a small Ontario town. There was only an 11 month age difference between him and his brother. Yet they were not close. His brother had a huge sex drive, sleeping with every female he could. (What was he trying to prove/ run from?) In a small town they should have shared friends. They were both into partying and recreational drug use--but not with the same friends.

When I arrived at their house to care for their handicapped sister, their mother told his brother, "Leave this one alone, this one is for your brother." This I heard after the fact of course. When I moved in with their family during my college years I was supposed to be given my own room. My Catholic parents were upset enough as it was that I was living there. Each night I'd go into my bedroom to find my soon-to-be mother-in-law in my bed reading (She suffers from insomnia). This woman, 40 years older than me, older than my parents even, would say, "Could you sleep with my son tonight? I can't sleep." In the morning she'd come down to get something out of the freezer, walk past us, smile and wave at us....and I'd turn red with embarrassment. Hindsight: I think she so loved to see her son in bed with a female, she would have taken a picture if she could have. I'd think, "Who was this woman, older than my parents that apparently supported premarital sex?"

My ex's friends would all tell me how much he'd changed since he met me. When I'd asked in what way--they'd say "for the better" and "his stutter had improved," but there was always this vagueness about it.

My ex told me one time this friend told him, "They'd love you in prison." This was in reference to his endowment. When I asked in what context this conversation occurred, he said it was after a big drunken party and this guy had done some time in jail. My ex and his brother were known to have big ones and their nicknames, "wiener" and "sausage" reflected that.

My ex's quote, "I can't give you what you need" was always meant as I can't/won't talk emotions and that's what I needed but can't have from him. In hindsight I think the quote should be "I can't get from you, a woman, what I need," but as was typical of my ex., "Let's spin this one a bit and make me feel like I'm unreasonable, too needy, too high maintenance." Very confusing to me because he used to let me talk feelings, and then for no apparent reason, he just stopped being willing to listen.

Each Thursday night my ex would go out to what he called "choir practice" with his coworkers. It was drinks after work for just a few hours. Many times I'd ask to attend as I was so isolated with young kids. I got a whole whack of excuses. "Spouses didn't really attend these things," he said.

No real explanation for why it's called choir practice either. One day I had a family emergency--he was not where he said they were. He denied it--said he was in that bar--its just that I didn't see the car out front because he'd parked it up on Queenston Street, where the gay bar happens to be located. This did not make sense that he'd park on Queenston--and I knew he was lying about the bar he was in as I had actually been inside looking for him and he absolutely was not there. At the time I let it go as the family emergency was unfolding.

While living with the in-laws, my mother-in-law, whom I'd been very close with, turned on me. She and my ex had many private talks down in their section of the house. My ex and mother-in-law watched a show on television together on gay people being cured. My ex came upstairs and told me about the show and of course asked me what I thought. In hindsight I believe my mother-in-law was punishing me for not curing her son. Or perhaps she was trying to drive me out of the house so that I'd flee and leave my marriage and her grandchildren behind.

Sex was like clockwork--two times per week in the beginning and once per month after our first child was born.

Extreme vanity--he'd get me to sew the sides of his jeans so they were tight, making his endowment apparent. He would not go out with me after work unless he had a clean pair of pants, yet he had a desk job and the first pants were just fine to me.

My ex had over 100 lovers before me. For someone so experienced, he had no idea what to do with BOOBS! I never critiqued for fear of hurting his feelings and ego.

He was incongruous in many ways. He said he loved me, was passionate about me. Yet I never felt truly loved by him. His actions were not in sync with the words he spoke. I thought he didn't know how to love, not having seen it at home.

Lack of affection--I soon found myself fishing for crumbs and compliments. I was systematically groomed to expect less and less from him and kept at arms length.

My acceptance of a "non-participating nothing husband" was not good enough for him. I did everything but was not allowed to discuss feelings or emotions with him. I tried to make it work, and he actively tried to make it not work. He was contrary to the point of trivial and ridiculous.

He'd say "I can't give you what you need". This confused me because he used to give enough-then just stopped for no apparent reason. He rejected me on so many levels and it left me baffled because I really cut him so much slack and made his life so easy.

When I was pregnant with our first child, my ever-so-lazy non-athletic husband joined a fitness club. Several clubs folded in the 80's taking our lifetime membership money with them. Yet still he was determined to belong to a fitness club at all costs year after year. Their washrooms must have been something else.

EXTRA NOTE: It doesn't have to be gay porn--any porn will do. My ex and my father-in-law would watch sexually explicit television in front of anyone--guests, our children. Just because there is a couple going at it on the screen doesn't mean your spouse is actually watching the GIRL!!!!

Blame Was the Name of the Game

He was bored with our sex life (Hah, I should have been the one to say this!!!!) He made me feel physically unattractive "You dress in flowers like your mother, you gained 30 pounds after 4 pregnancies," so I guess I married the heavy sister of your family. He refused to feed me emotionally for years offering no meaningful conversation or affection and then expected fireworks !!

He kept me so sleep deprived and exhausted from caring for our sleep-disordered handicapped child single-handedly, and he had me doing the lion's share of housework. I worked several jobs to pay the bills and accommodate his selfish expenses. And then he'd wake me up and ask for sex--having almost guaranteed that I was so exhausted my skin hurt. Then he could blame me for not wanting it.

He blamed me for my daughter's autism because, "Boy, you really did have to have that third child, didn't you?" The day we received her diagnosis he cut me off sexually for the remaining 6 years of our marriage because his "mind knows it's not my fault, but his heart still blames me" Ah, the perfect excuse for no sex and he could heap the blame at my feet. Me, being the perfect wife, (love is patient and kind and bears all things said the minister at our wedding)--decided to stick this out and prove that our daughter really was loveable and worthwhile. Someday he'd say he was sorry. "Someday." But he kicked me in the face instead.

He said our handicapped daughter was "sucking the life out of our marriage". Yet Whenever I arranged for care for her by trained staff, he'd pick a fight with me. He'd say he didn't like the other handicapped children there and blamed me for leaving her with them. He would stonewall me in silence for the entire respite weekend. We sent her to a treatment center and he had issues with the staff, causing more stress than it was worth, and we pulled her out. He wanted to hold onto that excuse that she was sucking the life out of our marriage for all it was worth.

He said I was "too emotional". When my grandmother died, I cried. He offered to take me to the psychiatric wing of the hospital. In 28 years I had never seen him cry. When I cried he'd get angry. I learned not to cry. He accused me of still being emotional underneath. If I was too emotional, he was an absolute flat liner. No pulse. I realize now that that was because he was never "in the marriage". He was under-emotional, distant and selfish.

Sex Tells It All

His excuses included:
- ✓ "I'm the laziest person I know"
- ✓ "I had so much sex in my teen years that I guess I've worked it out of my system" (by age 30)

✓ "I don't want to hurt the baby" (He used every pregnancy as a vacation from all sex and cuddling)

✓ "Sex on demand killed it for me. It took all the fun out of it and it stayed with me" (We had suffered a two year period of infertility while trying to conceive our second child).

✓ "I don't know if it even works anymore because of the medication I take for depression"

✓ "My parents stopped sleeping together by age 40. People don't do it all their lives" (My parents were active until they'd both had bypass surgery, in their 70's, they were afraid of literally killing each other in bed! The playful affection continues)

How I Caught Him

My second child was showing obvious aversion to her father in the months leading up to my ex's departure. She talked of moving somewhere where no one knows us and starting all over in a new school. This from a shy girl! Months later my ex said he was leaving for an old flame. My daughter had written him a letter but left on a five day school trip without leaving the letter out. In searching her room for this letter I stumbled upon her diary and journal. There was an entry called "You're So Stupid". "You're so stupid, you didn't graduate high school." (My ex had had to return and get his equivalent)

..."I saw you in the bathroom with that bloody razor" (I recall him borrowing a razor from me that I use to scrape algae off the aquarium several months before he dropped the bomb. I also recall pointing out band aids on his wrists saying it looked bad when he gave me some excuse)

..."I hear you go out at night and I know where you are going." (I work lots of overnight shifts so it's possible)...

..." That man I saw you kissing at the mall must be 15 years older than you"... (What would a 13-year-old know about age gaps in gay men unless from first hand knowledge?)

..."And the way you talk to mom is so mean and cruel"...

My mind immediately flashed back to five months prior when I was called to the local mall to pick up my daughter. She was hysterically crying. Her first words when she got into the car with her friend were, "Where's Dad?" He was at this mall running some errands. The story that she and her friend gave me sounded scripted. They said her friend's boyfriend had been in a knife fight. Yet her friend was calm and my daughter cried all weekend. My ex made a sudden departure out of town to care for his sick parents. My daughter had me searching in snow banks at the mall the next morning for the knife that was used (she said it was a butter knife!)

Okay, so I found my daughters journal. When I presented my ex with the diary page, he read it and reread it slowly in silence. There was no anger or indigence. No smashing of fists on the table. With a long pause he said "What did our daughter say?" as if gauging how "caught" he was. He denied anything happened at the mall. I had not talked to my daughter at this point as she was away, and any way, I was addressing him, not her! I said, "So what else could it be? Is your girlfriend such a woof burger that she could be mistaken for a man?" He denied that the girl had ever been to our town. I said "Okay, were you doing hot knives with a guy at the mall so it just looked that way?" He denied ever doing drugs at the mall. He said he had no idea what the diary meant.

When my daughter returned from her trip, she hysterically denied it as well. In 12 pages of truthful diary entries about the activities of her and her friends she was saying that those two lines about kissing a man were made up. It doesn't make sense. Her silence had been bought.

In subsequent diary entries there was huge anger, ominous stuff (like I'm about to explode so everybody better watch out), and 2 suicide letters. I took her for counseling and she wouldn't even get out of the car. The counselor couldn't get her out. She was hysterical and terrified to talk. She hasn't spoken to my ex in two years, and is sure she is done with him. Sure he will not be at her wedding in 5-10 years from now. She wants him dead. She is gleeful if he's a little late for picking her younger sister up for visitation because she hopes for a bad car accident. She hides behind bushes and trees outside and jumps behind furniture when he's at the door. She does not want him to get the pleasure of seeing her face. Within days of his departure, she said, "Go for sole custody mom, he's not even going to know me."

It is not the fear of the sexually abused child. She's laughing as she hides. It is pure contempt. She is happy and relieved he's gone. She's changed schools twice as if she wants to go where her past is not known, seeking a new identity. Her lavish birthday and Christmas gifts to me make me suspect she feels guilt.

When the word gay comes up in general conversation, she is quick to angrily say "It's a choice." Yet I'm sure that her peers are taught in school otherwise in this day and age.

For me, when I read my daughters diary, I felt the floor go out underneath me "like an elevator". It explained all the questions and inconsistencies in my relationship with my ex and his family. It all "fit."

I feel my son knows this on a gut level too. He's been suffering from depression since shortly after my husband left. He questioned his father if he was gay and got denials. The ex of course says "You're mother is crazy. She gets an idea in her head and just won't let it go."

My son says "Does anyone ever really know dad?" He's a stranger even to his kids who've been around him all their lives."

Happily Ever After – For Real!

While my ex was in the house, I was single parenting for years, doing everything myself except for the odd handyman thing. Now that he's gone I'm able to tackle the handyman things he left behind me without fear of emasculating him. And you know what--I'm a hell of a handyman. And I'm twice the parent he ever was. I am able to raise my teenagers the way I want to without anyone dragging me down. Life is just easier without him. House routines are a joy because now I do them out of love for my children--gone is the anger over having to do it "because he didn't".

For my children, I now have a working behavior management team handling my autistic daughters challenging behaviors. There is no more garbage on the television--which she imitates--only children's shows for her viewing. She no longer displays sexual mannerisms--no more complaining neighbors on my porch. The ex can watch his porn alone now.

My teens are very against pot and drugs because they've seen what it can do to a father. I'm raising smart teens in a drug free environment. The ex was very into escapism. The kids consider him a loser, who never even tried to be a good parent.

The old me is emerging--happy, joyous, and funny. The one that used to laugh HARD each day has reappeared after 2 decades of confusion and tears. I am at peace with my role in the marriage--I did everything I could think of and imagine to make it work--not really knowing that it was patently unworkable. I'll be a wonderful partner to someone who deserves me.

I have read many books including: _How To Avoid Marrying A Jerk_, Getting It Right This Time, and Bonnie Kaye's books on Dysfunctional Men and Gay Men. I know what I'm looking for. My ex complained that I never was one to initiate sex. It was the only way I could gauge whether this flat liner cared for me at all. I initiated with the boyfriend before him fine. And I know that I can initiate now with someone who is straight. I pinned my last date against the wall behind our garage and French kissed him ferociously—I'm going be just fine!

I have just dated a man who recently won 15 million in the lottery. He was very affectionate and I know he was straight. No gay man would engage in 3 hours of heavy petting in the blazing sun--the effort and enthusiasm and stamina would just not be there. In the end, I was turfed for not putting out all the way after three dates. He wouldn't talk to me like a person; there were no flowers and no wine and dining. I am looking for the real thing that money can't buy. My heart doesn't sell for cheap. I figure it was his loss. HE MISSED OUT ON THE BIG SURPRISE.

My ex always said my oral skills were the best he'd ever had. Knowing what I know now, that must mean I'm better than 100 gay men! I really must be talented then!

From Mr. 15 Million Dollar man I learned 12 things that I want or don't want in a man. I wrote it down to remind myself. In a nutshell, I learned that my body craves affection. Communication, respect, honesty and loyalty are important to me. I must be treated well and feel valued this time. I know what I'm looking for this time and I'll not settle for anything less. I know my worth and will not give myself away to someone who hasn't earned it. I'll save that secret little talent of mine for someone who is worthy--someone who I can love and trust who loves me equally in return.

Life is good. I have the love and respect of my children. They think I'm really cool because I don't do drugs and neither do they. We go to rock concerts together to make family memories. I'm enjoying their teenaged years as much as I did the newborn stages. Their friends come over to our house to hang out, play their guitars, and they are all really good kids.

My kids think that I should go out and meet an extraordinary man. They want that for me. I'm going to go out and find him! You betcha!!!

PROFILE #27: CATHY L. I'm divorced and have four children, ages 30, 24, 18, and 15. I own a beauty shop and I'm from Pennsylvania.

I had three men in my life that was gay, which is sad but true. The first one was so fine people told me he was gay, but I didn't believe that for one minute. Why would he want me so bad? I didn't spy on him--I just caught him with another man. The red flags I missed were he was bleeding every time he went too the bathroom, and one day, when I saw him bent over in the bathroom starting his bath, I could see his anal area was all stretched out. I was young and naive. When I caught him, I told him if he could prove to me he wasn't gay by a doctor, and then I would come back to him. He said okay he would go, but asked if the doctor said he's gay, will I come back? I said no, and that was the end of the relationship.

Gay man number two: I married a man that treated me like a queen. When I met Jim, I fell head over heels for him. I thought he was my knight in shining armor. I didn't get too see him much when we were dating because he lived over an hour away and worked the midnight shift. It was hard, and there wasn't much sex, but I wrote if off to his demanding work schedule.

One day, I met his best friend. My first thought was, "Oh my God-they're gay!" But I took that thought right out of my head. I thought the sex would change when we got married and he changed jobs. Then he had excuse after excuse… he was too tired… I was over sexed… he worked too hard. It just wouldn't work at all, so we went to the doctors to investigate the problem. They took some tests, blood work and all, but nothing was wrong with him. His levels of testosterone were through the roof. So then I started playing detective, and I hired one, too. 1,600 dollars later… the guy just took all my money for nothing. I got more information than he did. I put a voice recorder under the seat of his truck and boom--in one day he was busted. He was meeting men at road side stops, and I had a spy at his job that caught him in the act with a gay man. I had also had his underwear tested for semen--ten pairs… all had semen on them, but he couldn't get an erection with me.

I confronted him and he admitted what he did with men, but asked me to stay with him anyhow. I said, "No way, it doesn't work that way," and I sold my house and got a divorce.

Then I was on my own for over a year. My dad was dying, and I was so lonely. I went online dating. I fell for a guy that everyone said he was gay, but I didn't believe it for one minute. Well, we moved in together, and I was in love. We did everything together. The red flag was he wanted gay people dead and hated them with a passion. Every day he would say that, and here I came to find out that he was on line with men and women. He walked gay, talked gay, he never had oral sex with me, but he loved me doing him. He would wait until I was almost asleep and have sex with me from behind. He never made real love to me after the first time we were together. He would quit having sex with me for a month at a time, and he was always in a rage about something, acting like a mad man.

❖

PROFILE #28: MARGARET P., 52, Arkansas, married, divorced three times. Partner who came out was a live-in lover.

Sex Tells It All

After the end of a 15 year marriage, I met him through the Internet and dared to trust with my broken bleeding heart. It was the man that I had the courage to give what was left of my faith in love. He was 17 years younger my junior, but there was no reason for me to believe there was a difference between us bigger than our ages. He had been married and divorced twice before meeting me. Even with our age differences, we had several things in common. Our biggest struggle was that our sex life was problematic. At first he seemed to have a genuine passion for it, but eventually it became an unbalanced and frustrating situation for me. He had a problem with premature ejaculation and eventually, additional problems maintaining an erection during sex. Considering his age, I was concerned because he was way too young to experience problems like this without a medical reason. He assured me constantly that it was his fault and he was really sorry. However, he never elaborated on what he meant by "his fault."

I suggested, "Perhaps a trip to the doctor might not be a bad idea." In my mind, with today's medical advances, there was a good possibility we wouldn't have to continue to deal with the problems that had begun causing me a great deal of sexual frustration.

I tried not to make my sexual frustration apparent; however, I am not good when it comes to hiding my feelings or anything else for that matter. In between pushing for medical advice, I did my best to do all the things a woman can do to make it easier on our sexual relationship. I bought sexy lingerie to wear to bed. I set the mood with candles and aromatherapy. I made sure my kisses were sensuous and passionate. I concentrated on touching sensitively and gently. I was loving and kind. In spite of our attempts, our sexual moments still left me physically frustrated and emotionally negative. I felt lost, confused, and helpless. My life began to feel like I was living in an emotional vacuum and my confidence as a vibrant, sexy, attractive woman started to crumble.

I remember that Sunday morning in May 2004. I woke up as part of a couple and went to bed as a single woman. Since he started out by telling me that he was bisexual, I was a <u>hopeful</u> single woman. To me, bisexuality meant that I could still be part of his life in a sexually intimate way. But as the days and weeks went on, he told me that he was more gay than bisexual. Eventually, the word "Bi" dropped out of our conversations and never came back. Consequently, sex disappeared also.

We could see that we were good for each other without a romantic relationship, so we opted to sustain our friendship and rebuild it. However, it didn't come without the price of evolution and serious adjustment. Separating ourselves from each other has not been a pleasant experience. I felt disappointed, hurt, betrayed, and angry that our romantic relationship was over.

I vacillated emotionally something fierce. I bounced back and forth between sadness, pain, fear, despair, peace and understanding constantly. My only true peace was when I was sleeping.

My perception of him vacillated too with equal intensity. I loved him, I hated him, I liked him, I didn't trust him, I did trust him, I wanted to control him, I wanted to let go, and there were times when I didn't know what I wanted. I actually wanted it to all just go away, disappear with the same kind of magic that made it appear. The truth is, I wanted things to be "normal" again, but I knew it would never be the same. Instead, it was going to be a different "normal" and I could chose to be part of the new "normalcy" or not part of it. In order to feel some sense of sanity, I kept trying to reason with a situation that wasn't reasonable. I found levels of pain, sorrow, anger, and even numbness that I didn't know existed in me.

I couldn't understand how he could make love to me and be gay. Eventually I discovered that he was fulfilling a sexual role of what he believed things were supposed to be and it really didn't have anything to do with me.

We fought often and deeply. The same passion we once used to love one another now was being used to fight one another. Finally I told him we have to somehow find a different way to find resolution and compromise because the fighting was putting our friendship in danger.

Ground rules were set, mostly for my benefit as my anger felt out of control at times. I needed the rules to give me back my sense of "boundaries."

Since he came out of the closet, it has often felt like I went in and shut the door behind me. My sexuality has disappeared from my view. This isn't the first time that happened. After surviving constant sexual abuse as a child, my womanhood for the last thirty years has vacillated between promiscuity to sexual denial and back to promiscuity. I was never able to find a happy, content balance.

It has been very difficult for me to face how his denial of his homosexuality has forced me to pay with my own sexuality. It has been a devastating blow to my womanhood. I am not sure why that is – I am not appalled by the idea of sex with a gay man. In my mind, it somehow borderlines on "sexual abuse" because I feel and believe he was involved with me in a place where he didn't belong, and even if I didn't know that, he somehow did and he never should have put me in the position that he did. It is easy for me to see how I would think of it in those terms.

After all these years, I know with all certainty I am going to survive this situation. I know it is going to take time. I know that without the homosexual issue, he is a good man, and he truly didn't intend to hurt me. He needed someone he could trust and come out to, part of me is glad I could be there for him and part of me really hates that is where I was at the time.

I don't like being a victim and I don't intend to stay one, but for now, I am definitely afraid of loving and being loved intimately. I tell myself that is okay. It is okay to be afraid, it is okay to feel uncertain. For whatever reasons – it is okay. It is just plain OKAY. For now, Okay is the best place I can be for me.

PROFILE #29: RUBY C., UK. I grew up with my Mother, Susan, as my Father, Che, lived in Australia. My Mother is a good Mother and ensured that as a child I was always loved, well dressed and fed, and well educated. We had our own large house with a large garden. I had older sisters, Judy and Rosy and brothers, Michael and Joseph from my Mother's first marriage who had all left home by the time I was 5 years old. My Mother provided a stable home life for me and only worked within school hours so she was always there when I got home from school. My older brothers, both 20 years older than me, were the main adult males in my life otherwise I was surrounded by feminine but independent women, my Mother and My Aunts who lived nearby. All school holidays we went to stay with my older siblings and I became an older sister figure to their children and I got on well with my sister's husbands and my brother's wife.

Before I went out with my first husband, I had a few boyfriends but they were relationships of just a few weeks or months and didn't involve penetrative sex. I met my husband when I was 17.

Looking back and recognizing that I was living in a dominant white host country but from a minority ethnic group, I can see some commonality with my ex-gay husband who was gay deep down but living in a culture that overtly expresses itself as heterosexual. We both came from backgrounds that were different from the majority. I now wonder if on a deeper level this created an unconscious attraction.

After having my second child, I gave myself an opportunity to reconnect to life by going out with some friends on a girl's night out. My husband was happy about babysitting. I came back around 11 p.m., my oldest child asleep in the little nursery bed and my baby fast asleep in the cot. My husband was awake but sitting in darkness in the living room, listening to music and drinking alcohol. I walked cautiously into the living room knowing that something was wrong. This was unusual for him. I had noticed in between breastfeeding my baby and going back to work that he was becoming melancholy.

He looked at me with heavy eyes, a glass of whisky in his hand, his head close to the music playing from the music centre. I gingerly walked towards him and asked what the matter was. He got up from his chair and moved to sit down on one closer to me. I knelt in front of him waiting for his reply. He told me there was nothing the matter with me, and that I was beautiful and that he loved me. I was confused. I searched his face. We had everything we had planned to this point in our young lives. We were 29 years old, qualified professionals, had two lovely little children, a car each and a house with a garden that suited our needs. He just replied it was all to do with him but would say no more. He was depressed. I wondered if he had male post-natal depression, if there was such a thing.

Months passed and his condition appeared to increase. He went to work but his heart was heavy, the joy seemed to have gone out of our lives. Two lovely children and it was a time to celebrate them. I held my children close to my heart and protected them. At weekends he would lay in bed with stomachache. I then stepped into being the entertainer for my children and took them on outings he sometimes attempted to raise himself to join us. By then, with no expression from him of his woes, I began to feel resentful. It seemed so unfair. I knew I was a good wife and a good Mother but he was clearly unhappy, it all was clearly not enough for him. I felt sad too in my heart, I wept and could feel my heart ripping, as I carried on with everyday life. He seemed to be up as well as down, I just knew he was not acting as the loving husband he had been.

I tried to be compassionate and patient with him. I would greet him from work with a smile and show an interest in his woodwork night class. I visited it once as a surprise; normally he would have been happy to see me but instead he was furious that I had arrived to meet him. I was most definitely hurt, but he didn't seem to care. I could not understand what was going on. He had always shown he cared for me, always been ready to protect me like it was us against the world. Now he seemed irritated by my presence, no longer melancholy just irritated and dismissive of me. It was time to try and find out.

I was sure there must be someone else, so I asked him was there someone at work. I pondered over the women he worked with which he might find attractive but he denied there was anything with anyone. I did believe him. I then began to think it must be me. Maybe I was worn out with working part time and caring for two little children, but he said no, it was not me. I returned to my suspicions that it might be his health and went to an herbalist and bought him ginseng. He thanked me and took it. He did seem to have more life but not towards me.

Things were not the same as they had been and never were again. His birthday arrived and I decided to push myself to make an effort for him, even though I was feeling deeply sad and unnerved. I made a cake with my two little children and we excitedly got food together to make an attractive birthday tea set out in the dining room. My children were excited and giggly at wishing Daddy 'Happy Birthday.' We had the cake all ready with candles ready to light. We waited and we waited but he didn't arrive. My heart sank. My children were hungry and so we had to eat. He arrived looking slightly embarrassed and as though it was unusual that I should have prepared a birthday tea for him. In all our 12 years together, by then, we had always celebrated occasions and made a special effort. This small offering of a birthday tea at home was not out of the ordinary it was all I could muster as I struggled to comprehend what was happening to our relationship.

After that night when I found him sitting in the dark with a glass of whisky another 9 months passed. I was in limbo and extremely confused, but certain that he knew what was the matter with him. He seemed to be focusing on wanting to find himself and it seemed a deep private search. He began to read a lot. My older male work colleague across the road was a good friend to me and seemed to recognize that my husband needed a friend. They went out for drinks together and began sharing literature. At first I was happy as hopefully this friendship would make him happier. Keith lent him novels to read. I asked what they were about. They were all gay novels. My husband liked literature and so did I. I felt perturbed by such a focused interest, but he tried to pass off my unspoken concern by justifying that it was good to be open-minded and that it was expansive to read about different ways of life.

As well as being friends with Keith, I was also friends with his wife Mary. She knew I was concerned about my husband so we planned for a day out, to relieve me of the worry. We took both our sets of children and planned a route in the country where we could push the toddler's carriages. It was lovely walking under the fresh summer branches with warm sunlight shining through the leaves. The children were happy and toddled along breathing in the fresh air. I had good talks with Mary and we discussed how her husband was also melancholy at times and agreed that it must just be men.

When we arrived back on our street, my husband was there to greet us in the front garden. He seemed to want to display that he had been working very hard and showed me all he had done on the garden. Part of me wanted to feel joy that maybe all we needed was a breathing space but my other senses told me things were still not right. Why was he so keen to show me everything he had done? It was as if he was trying to prove it to me.

He had made another male friend at a literature night class whilst I was expecting our second child. Paul and his girlfriend became part of our lives and they too had a child. My husband continued to be in contact with Paul and described how having a friend like him was like having the brother he had never had. I was confused. I had good female friends but it was if he was discovering friendship with the same gender for the first time. He had had lots of male friends at University but never spoken about them like this. It didn't make sense.

Gradually I processed and eliminated all that could be wrong with him and my attention turned to one of the gay novels lying by our bed side. It was constantly there every day and I began to wonder. One night we were lying in each other's arms after having had sex. We were close. We were holding each other and it felt safe, safe to broach the unspoken. Steadily I told him that I knew that something was still wrong and I asked him:

"You don't want to have sex with another man do you?" Instantly he burst into tears and lay his head on my breasts. I was rigid with shock and a sharp current of energy shot through my body. My eyes were wide as I recognized danger. We cried in each others' arms, I knew I had unraveled the mystery but I so wished it wasn't true.

When I look back the signs I noticed were his change in behavior, becoming irritated and dismissive of me and drinking alcohol heavily. Overcompensating was also a sign such as my husband doing excessive gardening but wanting to make sure that I saw it I now think that this was to 'cover the tracks' as he had probably spent time with another man whilst I was out. His new interest in gay literature coupled with everything else that had begun to unnerve me and shake the foundation of our relationship was the final thing that made me begin to realize.

The final straw was one night when he stayed out all night, my children came into me early in the morning asking where he was. He arrived home around 5:00 am and tried to hug me. I could smell the scent of another man, I pushed him away. He was hurt. A few weeks later I told him I wanted him to move out. This was painful but in the two years after I found out he was gay it was the best thing I ever did for myself, for him and for our children.

Revelations and Assurance That I Did the Right Thing in Separating

It is now 18 years since the night that I knew things were changing. Over a period of a year our relationship began to dissolve after that night. We went through a period when he swore me to secrecy. His disclosure that he was gay was our secret. It was like sitting on a time bomb. I suffered internally and began to have extremely heavy menstruation that had to be controlled by medication. Always a thin young woman I lost more weight. People expressed concern but I had promised not to tell. I was very, very unhappy but went to work looked after my children and I reengaged with my childhood passion of art. I realize now my own resilience and strength. I rang the national gay helpline, the man told me every week they had a few calls like mine, from wives. He urged me to press my husband to come out.

I told my husband I had rang. He was angry. I told him I couldn't hold the secret any longer. I told him I needed him to be clear, was he really gay? I urged him to work out if he was. I needed and deserved the truth. I needed to know what I was dealing with. He began going out to gay night clubs while I stayed in with the children. He became more and more arrogant and more and more dismissive of me. Slowly, slowly I began to draw together my inner strength knowing that I could not 'be' in this situation. Sometimes my memory of our loving relationship in the past and the longing for it let me down. When I made myself face the present I knew I couldn't stand for it; I knew it was not what I wanted.

About five years after I discovered my husband was gay, his supposed friend who he had said was like the brother he never had told me that he and my husband had slept together and had had a sexual relationship. I rang my ex husband about it but he denied it. Paul was clear that it had happened. I never found out if there had been anything between my husband and another friend Keith who lent him gay literature, but what I know is that Keith and his wife Mary moved away and didn't keep in touch. I sometimes wonder how Mary is.

Sometimes I wonder what else I didn't know but now I am much more interested in concentrating on my life. Whatever else happened that I don't know about is now irrelevant as what is important is that I know I did the right thing in separating from him and what I learnt five years after we separated just confirmed it for me. My husband had been angry with me that I wanted to separate and was even angrier when I had my first relationship a year later. Strange as by then he had been living with his gay lover for over a year!

How I Began to Grow and Forgive

Years and years of gradually accepting what had happened and years and years of working on myself and rebuilding my self-confidence, confidence in myself and in men, I feel I have moved on enormously. Since then I have changed careers, set up my own business and earned several university degrees. I've had some great sexual relationships with men and about 10 years ago began to realize that deep down I wanted to trust a man enough to marry again. In a pattern of being in unsettled relationships with men it took me a while to find the right man and then to recognize that I had. My new husband and I have a co-empowering relationship; we support each other in our dreams and we make dreams together. My children, now adults, can also plan to travel more and to expand our career horizons and it gets better every day.

I look back now and remember those painful years when we split up and the heartache and disruption that followed. I also think of how our life would had been if we stayed together, and I know I would have become like a walking ghost. Now I am a confident woman with a loving husband. I no longer have contact with my ex-husband but I forgive him. Forgiveness is something that I did not feel I could achieve in the early days, as I was so hurt and mortified. My life felt like a nightmare.

Over the years I have begun to learn more about myself. As I felt so devastated about what had happened in my first marriage I realize that I didn't hear what people said to me about how well I had done. Now I do hear them more. I think for a long time I blamed myself not because I thought I could have caused him to be gay but because I didn't spot it before we got married and had children. Now I forgive myself because I was innocent in all senses of the world. I had only heard of pop stars being bisexual and I had never heard of married men seemingly becoming gay, of course maybe they were just gay all the time and either had kept it a secret or just didn't want to recognize they were. I know that I truly went into my first marriage in trust and innocence. I was a loyal loving and beautiful wife. It is so great now that I can be all those things to my second husband and that he appreciates me and wants what we have together.

What I have also begun to recognize about myself is that I am a fine woman of substance and integrity. I also know that I am intelligent and wise. I know I was wise enough to quit my first marriage for the safety and happiness of myself and my children. It gave me a lease of life to expand, grow and achieve. It also feels satisfying that my ex gay husband was able to actualize who he really was.

I see little point in anyone of us in the beautiful life being dishonest to ourselves or others. If there are gay men out there who are not being honest about being gay to a loving female partner or wife I would urge them to be honest and tell the woman in their lives. To live dishonestly is unfair all around. It is especially unfair and shameful to the woman in a gay man's life and it is also unfair to them. For the sake of humanity I ask all gay men if they have a woman in their lives to be honest with her allow her and yourself to be free.

PROFILE #30: MAUREEN A., age 57, California. Married 26years, divorced nine years. I have three adult children. I had no experience before him. I married when I was 20, and after three months, I was pregnant. I didn't like him that much at first, but my love grew for him.

Red Flags I Missed

1. He started using a cell phone. This was a man that absolutely HATED phones.
2. I found videos in the garage, later to find out they were gay porn.
3. He never liked any of my woman friends.
4. He didn't know one thing about using a computer, but he learned real fast. When I would walk in the room he would click it off. Little did he know I was smarter than he thought I was. I managed to find everything. I took the computer out of the house and hid it. Some of these guys leave things in plain sight so you will see it, so they can be spared of having to tell you.
5. He left gay magazines in the car, the videos, names and addresses in plain sight for me to see.

The day before I confronted him he made me a card on the computer with a lion on the front. On the inside, he told me that he would love me forever. I was the only one for him.

Blame Was the Name of His Game

He blamed me for the whole thing, for ruining his life and every little thing he could blame me for. It took a good therapist to convince me that this was not my fault. He wrote me a long letter, telling me I controlled him. This was a bunch of garbage pointing the finger at me. He was very controlling, especially about money.

My husband was one of those men who worked every day, came home, read, ate dinner a little TV and then to bed. EVERY SINGLE DAY for 25 years, so when I saw the extreme change in him is when I started "my investigation."

PROFILE #31: Heidi B., 44, New York. Married 15 years, separated. Five children, Nurse. I grew up in the Caribbean the first 6 years of my life. My parents seemed to have a good marriage. When I was almost seven, my family moved to New Jersey, but my father stayed behind to sell his business. My mom had to go back to work, so my grandmother moved in to help raise my brother and me. She was a very negative person, never had nice things to say and would lecture for hours at a time. We were a fairly religious family; we went to church and youth group, and mom sang in the choir. My parents ended up divorcing when I was 12. She remarried when I was 14, basically to make sure my brother had a male influence. I did not date at all in junior high, and only had about 1 boyfriend a year in high school. They were all normal, no high achievers or dirt bags. I didn't date much in college either, was having too much fun with groups of friends. I graduated nursing school still not dating much. There were not a whole lot of men I was interested in, and those I was interested in did not want to date me. I met my husband when I was 28. I was a nurse at a boys' camp for a week where he was also working for the summer. He was a good Christian, had ambitions, and seemed to have a good family. He was also handsome, and we got along very well. We dated four months and got married nine months later. We were both virgins. I never would have guessed in a million years what lay ahead. My mother did ask me once, "Are you sure?" I said yes not giving it a second thought until the truth was revealed. My mom had passed on one year into our marriage, so I can't ask her why she asked me that question - did she suspect something wasn't right or do all mothers ask their daughters that question?

Hindsight is 20/20. I now realize my self-esteem SUCKED from about the time I moved to New Jersey. Dad leaving us and Grandma's constant belittling took its toll. Only in the last month or two have I realized that and have been working at it. I feel my Low Self-Esteem was the cause of not dating much, then taking everything that happened in my marriage personally. I can't help but wonder if my self-esteem was better if I would have been able to see clearer, sooner and gotten out sooner. Oh well!

Red Flags

When I met my husband, I thought God had made the perfect man. He was handsome, considerate, in the seminary, with a very supportive family. Things seemed to be terrific until I got pregnant with my first child, although, looking back there were signs I could see as far back as my honeymoon. He only wanted to have sex in bed, never more than once, and in one position - missionary. Every time I asked to try another position he said no, except occasionally I could be on top. I asked him if I could give him oral sex once and he looked horror stricken - as if he were going to vomit.

Blame Game

Of course everything was my fault. My mother died shortly after my first son was born. We were very close so everything was blamed on me not getting over mom's death fast enough. Later, my mother-in-law blamed me because I didn't love him enough. PHOEY!

Sex Tells It All

Before I got pregnant he was all for having sex once a night. After I got pregnant, he rarely wanted to have sex. He would stay at work late or watch television until late and he was sure I fell asleep (being pregnant and later having an infant that didn't take long). The only way he seemed willing to have sex was to have another child. As time went on, he never kissed me except for little tight lipped kissed that lasted a nanosecond, and only if there were an audience. If there was no one there to see his "display of affection," there weren't any. Because I was a virgin when I got married, I started to think there was something wrong with me and the way I was performing. I was doing something wrong and not meeting his needs. I spent a FORTUNE on lingerie, how to books and DVD's. Nothing helped.

How I Caught Him

One day when my self-esteem was at an all time low--as in suicidal ideations low--a friend came over. He asked what was wrong and I started purging- and purging and purging. When I finally took a breath he looked at me and said, "It's not you!" That thought never entered my mind before. But it was like a light bulb went off, like a ton of bricks came crashing off my shoulders. My mind started clearing and I started listening to my sixth sense, which had been screaming at me for some time, but I ignored. My husband was doing something he shouldn't have been. My brother told me he thought my husband was gay, but I blew him off, thinking, "Okay, if he's gay, that would answer a lot, but it's not really true." He couldn't be gay--he was a youth pastor.

We had four boys and an adopted daughter. I started to see where he had been lying to me, about times where he was supposedly at someone's house but wasn't. He always could say someone called him for a problem. I started to not believe him.

I put an electronic tracking device on his car. It was an okay device; it told me the general vicinity he was in and what times but it wasn't specific. There are many better devices and programs now. I inadvertently found pictures of nude men in his bedside table. I could no longer keep the thought he was gay at the back of my mind. I confronted him, and he said they were from one of the teenagers he was working with. Ha! I wasn't the only one who was suspicious of his behavior.

His secretary at work put a spy program on his computer at work. I went to my father- in- law about the pictures to ask for help, and he believed my husband, that they were some kid's. Four days later he was arrested for child pornography. The charges were ultimately dropped to a lesser charge because no one could prove the boys were really under 18. The arresting officer told me he had confessed to having affairs and oral sex, which really infuriated me because he led me to believe it was repulsive. I stayed with him for a while for the kids but couldn't stand the lie. I have since filed for divorce.

When I found out he was unfaithful, I knew I needed help. I went straight to my primary physician to be tested for every STD under the sun (even though later I was told that wasn't necessary because he practiced safe sex - liar), got a prescription for sleeping pills and stomach pills. I found a local counselor and then - thank God! – Bonnie Kaye.

Happily Ever After

The biggest relief was knowing that IT WASN"T ME! I wasn't unattractive, I wasn't bad at sex, I wasn't a bad wife that didn't know how to love. There is nothing wrong with me - I'M NORMAL! While at this point in time I don't ever want to be tied to another man, I do want a friend to be intimate with in the future and have a normal relationship.

PROFILE #32: TRACY R., 42 years old and separated. I'm working on a divorce. I live in New York City. My favorite question is, "Did you know he was gay when you married him?" Well, duh, if I had known that he was gay, would I have married him? I guess some people would have answered "yes" to that question, but not me.

How I Caught Him

After months of speculation and suspicion, I started to check things out on my husband's e-mail account. He didn't know about those handy little "saved mail," "recently deleted" and "mail you've sent" folders on AOL. Until he figured that out, tracking his online activity was relatively easy. It also helped that I had Jeff's password for his AOL screen name.

Once he figured out how to delete his history online, I had to get more creative. It's good to have smart friends! One friend, in particular, is a computer programmer for a major publication. She installed software on my computer that took snapshots of the computer screen every 30 seconds. It also recorded all keystrokes and websites visited. It was through this software that I found out a great deal of information.

Jeff loved to brag to one particular friend during Instant Messaging conversations about his escapades. The software allowed me to see exactly what he wrote. I knew everything he was up to on business trips, trips to visit his parents, and local trysts. I would confront him with what I knew, and not tell him how I knew. To him it was mind-boggling; to me it was entertaining to watch him squirm. Of course, it was also incredibly hurtful, especially when he'd talk about me as if I were a weight hanging around his neck cutting off his oxygen. IF ONLY!!!

One night, Jeff and I went to a marriage counseling session with my therapist. I guess he saw her as his confessor because he came clean about all of his antics from the beginning of our marriage. He figured I knew what he was up to lately; he might as well come clean about the rest.

Even though we are now separated and working toward a divorce, I still have all computers in my house bugged. When he's here with the kids, there's no trusting him around the computers. He's been behaving himself lately after I caught him on my PC checking out gay porn. I guess he finally figured out that I can always stay one cyber-step ahead of him!

The Truth Behind His Lies

There were so many lies that it's hard to know where to start. Something as simple as, "I'll be right back, I have to go to the men's room," turned into a sexual encounter with some guy who happened to feel the need to relieve himself at the same time. Walking the dog also seemed to provide opportunity, as my husband felt perfectly comfortable and apparently safe giving more than directions to a man who stopped to ask how to get to a specific destination.

Having lied about finishing college, and then promising to complete his degree after we were married, my husband signed up for two classes. He dropped one, but failed to mention that fact to me. He did, however, stay out to create the illusion that he was attending both classes. It wasn't until he got his grade report in the mail and I asked to see it did he "fess up" to the fact that he withdrew from one of his courses. To this day I don't know how he used that time, but I do have my suspicions. At this point, I'd rather not know.

Vacations were always fun, especially when we were visiting family in Florida. He'd tell me he was going out for some errand, and go check out the gay bars and/or bath houses. He'd visit similar places while he was away on "business."

One of my favorite examples of his stupidity led to his brother finding out that he was gay before I had the pleasure of outing him. Jeff went to march in the Gay Pride Parade one year not knowing that his brother was in the city with his wife that day. My sister-in-law called later that day to say hello and see what we were up to. Jeff said he wasn't up to anything much, that he just hung around the house all day. It was then that my sister-in-law and brother-in-law put it all together. They had seen him marching in the parade, and as soon as he chose to lie about how he spent his day, they knew that he wasn't just there to support his co-workers!

PROFILE #33: ANNE H. New Jersey, Married 30 years, separated one year, but still living in same house with him. Six children, homemaker.

Sex Tells It All

I was only 17 when I married my husband. I got pregnant and figured that was the best thing to do. We only knew each other for a year before getting married, and he was only the second man I had ever been with sexually, so I was not experienced with sex. I had what I thought was a normal sex drive, but it seemed like I was the only one to initiate sex with my husband. I started to think I was oversexed. And even when I would try to initiate it, he would always have some excuse like he had a headache or upset stomach or felt too tired. I felt so rejected and so hurt inside. I then started to get angry with him and we would wind up in a big argument in bed. One time I put my arm around him and started to rub his back and other areas figuring this will get him aroused...well I was wrong! He grabbed my hand and threw it off him and hollered at me to leave him alone because he was trying to sleep. This happened a lot. I just kept trying because I needed to be wanted and desired.

Some nights I would just lay there and cry because I felt so hurt, rejected and frustrated, and he would roll towards me and rub my back, but never did he ask what's wrong. I couldn't understand why. I tried talking to him about it and he would say "I'm not a machine--I work all day!"

Two years into the marriage he had four or five guys come over from work to play cards and they were drinking. Later after most of them left, one guy stayed and I went to bed. I woke up and didn't see my husband next to me, so I went to see where he was. When I walked into the den there he was laying naked with the a guy in a 69 position, it was dark because the lights were out but it looked as if they were stroking each others penis, and they were both drunk and all I remember is my husband saying, "Hi honey, come on in." I was in shock and just turned and walked away and went back to my room.

The next day I asked him why he was doing what he was doing, and he said, 'I don't know--I was wasted and didn't know what I was doing." I figured it was because he was so drunk, and we never really spoke much about it again.

Years went by, and I had baby after baby and still lived in a sexless marriage, depressed and lonely. I didn't know what was wrong with me. Why didn't he desire me? I tried everything over the years. I bought these books called "Light Her Fire" and "Light His Fire," but he never touched the books, refusing to read them. I ordered, "How to Have an Affair Proof Marriage" on audio so he could listen to the book because I thought he didn't have time to read. He NEVER touched the tapes. I felt so helpless and hopeless. I just took care of my children and went on living like that all my 30 years with him.

One time about 15 years ago, I started to sleep on the couch, and I wouldn't go up to bed. I would ask, "Do you want me to come up to bed with you? He would say, "Only if you're coming up to sleep!" So I just lay on the couch and cried and cried. I was on that couch for two years. I went into a bad depression and gained about 50 pounds. I still don't know till this day how I got myself out of that rut and off the couch, but I did and I lost the weight.

My family tried so hard to help me out of that rut, and whatever they said did help me. I started to have a girl's night once a week at my house and a few of my friends were talking about their sex lives and how often the get sex or how much their husbands wanted it but they didn't. I sat there just thinking what is normal, and I asked how many times a week they had sex. Most said two or three times a week. One said four or five times a week. And I must have had this shocked look on my face because they said, "How many times do you have sex?" I started to stutter and said maybe once every four to six months. They said, "WHAT?" And I said, "Why that's not normal is it?" And they said, "NO!" Well that girl's night was 20 years ago!

Then we moved to a bigger house, and I got my first job at Home Depot and I loved it so much. Most of the employees were MEN! And they were all so nice and very flirty with me. I thought to myself what are they looking at? My husband never was this way to me. I felt like I was in another world. I loved getting up and going there because the men made me feel like a woman and I felt alive and so happy! I started having a relationship with a man there and it turned into a passionate affair. I never felt this way with my husband. The sex was fantastic. We were going to motels at least three times a week. I never knew how wonderful sex could be until I met this man. He was also unhappily married. It lasted for about eight months and I broke it off. I always felt so guilty for what I was doing. That was seven years ago. I got laid off from the job and became a homemaker again--and depressed again. But I now knew that I was an attractive woman and there were men out there who desired me.

It's really hard to tell all of my 30 unhappy years with my husband in a short amount of time. I never caught my husband with any more men in these 30 years. I think he is gay but doesn't want to be gay. He has an identical twin brother who has always been gay. And this year I found out one of my daughter's is gay. I've asked him many times if he was gay, and he says no. Also about 10 years ago, he agreed to be checked at an urologist for his low sex drive--No sex drive is what I called it-- and the doctor tested him for everything and all was normal.

The doctor gave him a prescription for Viagra, but my husband had no interest in taking it. The one time he did take it he got an erection, but it didn't give him a sex drive so it was useless! I even got someone to get me an adult sex film, but he didn't want to watch it with me. He just went along with what I tried to do to help our marriage so I'd leave him alone. I wrote him letters every few years begging him to talk to me and telling him how I needed to be desired and wanted by him, but he never responded. I started to go out with my girlfriends to a local bar and I met a wonderful man who I became close with as friends; then after two years of our friendship we started to have a relationship and I feel like I have never felt in my life. I love this man so much. All I can say is there is LIFE out there--love and passion like I have never felt in my life! A life I thought was never possible is possible! I plan on being with this man the rest of my life. So never give up hope like I did and don't wait 30 years to find it because our years are so valuable and there is so much I missed by waiting so long.

My husband would act differently with me around people when we were at a party or cookout. He would put on this act like he wanted me and would say, "Wait till we get home tonight honey." But of course when we got home and went to bed, it was nothing as usual. I hated when he did that and for years I would just smile and say nothing. I'm sure they thought he was serious but I was always too embarrassed to tell anyone it was all an act. I finally got so tired of him doing that, and I started to give my comments back to him in front of our company. I would say, "Yeah right, I wish!" and then I even got bold enough to say, "Don't believe this act he's putting on because when we do get home he wants nothing to do with me in bed!" He didn't like me saying that at all, but I did and he finally stopped putting on his show in front of them.

There were a few times we went away because I thought it would help our sex life and again NOTHING! At a hotel all alone, I brought sexy lingerie to wear and he'd get into bed roll over with his back toward me like he always slept when we were in bed and I'd try to get something going and he would snap at me and say, "Is that all you think about?" Anytime I'd try and talk with him he would get mad and yell at me, always saying he wasn't a machine and he worked all day. Or he'd say, "It's your mouth that makes me never want you." meaning I was nagging him.

❖

PROFILE #34: ANNIE M. My name is Ann Elizabeth hence the AnnE. I had a somewhat normal upbringing. My dad worked in NYC while my mom stayed at home. I have one sister and two brothers, one 4 years older and the other 4 years younger. There is four years between all of us. We were a close family and became closer when tragedy hit. My mom passed away in February 1965 after I had just turned 13.

Even though I had the responsibility now of practically running a household at a young age, I still did everything that teenage girls did. My father was my hero. That man is so high on my pedestal nothing could make him step down. My older sister, Elene, didn't spend that much time with us; after all she was a newly wed and learning her life with her husband.

My father was a very fair man and life changed for all of us. Dad would travel from time to time with his job but he no longer did since he had us at home alone. Lord knows he was a patient man and yes a religious man. He never hit us if we acted up, we'd stop instantly just by a look.

Outside of not having my mom, I had a complete and full childhood including my brothers. We never wanted for anything, we may have had to wait but that always made it appreciated that much more. I had met Pete, going to both my junior and senior prom with him. Pete was very good to my dad, he had to be or I'd kill him. When we talked about getting married after his time in the Navy, my dad had tears in his eyes and he used the same line on Pete that he did with my sister when she got married. I never hit my daughter and if I find out you did, you'll be buying gloves for one hand. Can we say protective of his girls?

When I moved up here in Albany with Pete, dad called me every Wednesday night and I called him every Saturday night. How he cried when I told him I was going to have a baby. The morning I gave birth, I couldn't talk, I cried trying to tell him he had a beautiful granddaughter with red hair; my dad was a red head. I cried, he cried, and Pete took the phone, laughing at us telling him all the particulars of the baby. "What a pair you two are," he said.

I have the best mother-in-law one could ever ask for. She is as heartbroken as I am. She is the mother I never had. If anyone could ask for a substitute mom, she is it. I could sit and talk to her and I knew it would stay with her alone. She still calls me and I call her. I get the most beautiful cards from her and they are always for a daughter-in-law. Yes, I have seen her since we broke up, at my daughter Catherine's graduation and last year for her 80th birthday when they gave her a surprise party.

Red Flags

When the lights went out for the life I had, not only was it dark but lonely and scary. I did my own mourning for a life that ended. Slowly, hour by hour turned into day by day, and I started doing things for me. One day, when I least expected it, the lights came back on, a beacon of light flashed before me like a lighthouse guiding in a ship lost in fog and rocky waters.

My story takes a different road than most yet spills into the same cesspool we all share. I was married for 27 years, living as brother and sister for the last twelve years of it. There was no sexual contact between us as he had me thinking there was a medical problem but yet was too proud to go to the doctors. I would ask for a hug and he shrugged at me. Finally, I stopped asking and I stopped wanting; I shut off all feelings.

The computer became an issue. Pete became selfish, a child who would not share, getting up hours before work to sign on with me not bothering him. I would walk into the room and the screen shut down to be glared at until I left. It became a game, how many times can I interrupt him. "And how is the whore today?" The computer replaced me, joking during chats as we once experienced a lifetime ago.

I had no clue nor any thought of Pete wanting the love of a man. I went home one day and thought I was robbed. Pictures were taken off the walls while empty hooks left told a sad story, furniture was taken and what was left was moved. The computer was gone with a shrine of dust where it once rested. I was robbed but by own husband. I was so naive and gullible; I thought I'd been left for a woman. The depression I felt was greater than what I had felt before as he laid his body next to mine each night, not getting a peck of a kiss good night, hell I was lucky if he patted my hand like one would a pet.

When I Caught Him

We do have one child, a girl, my breath. She was graduating college and this mama bear was so proud of her cub Things were tight as I'm living on one salary, starting my life over. I saved for months, going without to put money aside because she deserved this. I sent e-mail after e-mail with no response from Pete about what he wanted to do. Again I did what I knew best--I went ahead without him. Invitations went out and one to him also, I was going to have a brunch at my house after the ceremony. I rented a car for that weekend and made several trips, one was picking up our nephew at the airport and bringing him up to the college so he could be with her, they are only a few months apart in age. I went up with an empty car, just the two of us, coming home with space only for the driver. The rule was whatever fit in the car came home with me.

When the sun shined that morning, I was up. The house was ready and the food was ready. A friend will come over and warm the food. Strawberries were coated in powdered sugar waiting for the pouring of champagne. I waited for the buses with the graduates as the ceremony was off campus and they were coming together. Just as the buses started unloading the graduates and our nephew, I saw Pete walking towards us. I took a deep breath, an inner voice said, "Win that Academy Award, this was her day and her day only."

My friend Mary, I should say our friend, asked who was with Pete--I never saw him before. As he talked to a few in the group, ignoring me (what else was new) this man walked up to me, extended his hand, and introduced himself. I shook his hand and said, "I'm Annie, the mother of the graduate." After all, he was with the father of the graduate, and I still had yet to be acknowledged. He screeched, "Annie, I've heard so much about you, I'm so glad to meet you." Instantly I knew, I stepped back, my own arms hugging me. I tried to stop the tears, my body shook. Arms went around me from behind, it was my daughter. "Mom, its okay, I love you." I had to get away, I couldn't breathe.

Sadly I don't remember much of the graduation until the called my daughter's name, I jumped, whistled, hooted and hollered. She turned, waived and blew me a kiss. People thought my tears were for her, they were in a way, why did he choose that day, her day. My friend said "come with me" walking to the main floor standing on the side. She lectured me. "His timing sucks, you worked so hard, hold your head up high damn it and be proud. Shame on him and the air he breathes, this was not your doing. He's the coward; you are the hero. You wanted answers, you now have them." It took a few minutes for the words to sink in; she was right. Slowly my eyes dried, my hands stopped wringing along with the shaking. A strange calm came over me. All that time I thought it was me. I wasn't smart enough, wasn't pretty enough, wasn't anything for him, and now it wasn't about me, it was him.

Yes my dear friends, he brought him to the house for the party. I don't remember much besides throwing up many times. The champagne toast took a new meaning. "As a chapter in life closes, a new one begins. Enjoy the journey." This was my toast to my daughter and good bye to Pete. When I said the words his head turned toward me, I winked at him and took a sip, he knew. Later when I was outside smoking (I was outside a lot) Pete approached me. The words came out of my mouth. "Why, you at least owed me the truth," with his reply "I owe you nothing." I was physically and emotionally drained. Again smoking, his man came to me to thank me for inviting him, trying to hug me. I took a step and said, "I didn't." Then I turned to Pete and told him, "Don't darken my doorstep again." It was my time to turn my back and walk away, closing the door.

The sadness I experienced before was nothing compared to the depression I went into. I just didn't care. With these feelings I knew I needed help and eventually sought help. I can only tell you, I dreaded going. I use to come out, sit behind the wheel of the car and sob; I don't know why, sometimes I was sitting in the driveway and don't remember driving home. I was told I had to forgive to be healed. Pete made my whole life, all those years, a lie and I had to forgive. Damned with being healed, it would be a cold day in hell before I forgave.

This is how I found out about my spouse. It was on that day when, in my own eyes, I became a widow, my husband died. The Pete I knew and loved was gone. No longer was I the bearer of shame. I vowed to live the remainder of my life, the way I wanted. I would do for me. I read in a book that living well and looking even better was the best revenge one could have.

There is life after the demise of a marriage, and I am living proof. Simple things such as a bubble bath in the afternoon on a day off are a better gift to oneself than a pouch full of diamonds. The peace, the tranquility one feels is indescribable. Possessions that Pete took no longer are an issue; that is in my past; I am in my present and look forward to the future. You see, I have met a man, a real man, who takes my breath away when he even looks at me. I blush like a teenager when he whispers in my ear when we are out in public. I no longer ask for hugs, his arms are always open. I experience more with him in the short time we have been together than I did with my spouse all those years. I am laughing once again; a real laugh, not a mechanical chuckle. My heart is lighter now. It was and is a rocky road, trying to forget the past with thoughts clouding your judgment; trusting once again is such a major issue but when the beacon of light shines upon me, it pulls me back to the present from my past.

The past will forever be in our most inner thoughts--certain words even certain sounds and smells, will trigger a memory; some good, some not so good. Unfortunately, we can not turn off these emotions but they do fade in time. I hated hearing the words "time will heal." The hairs on the back of my neck would tingle. I remember tears rolling down my face only to drip off the chin making the chest wet thinking, "I do not want time, I need now, I need to stop hurting now." Why is it that each day or each week there was a different hurt?

I dislike the saying "eating crow," but right now that is what I am doing. Time does heal and it does lessen the pain. After all these years (shame on me) I decided to clean out the chest the computer sits on. I had no idea what was in there, but right on top of my daughter's baby books with records were papers. Opening them and reading them, did my hands shake? No. Did tears fall? No. My head went back and I laughed the deepest belly laugh one could ever experience. You see these papers belonged to my husband, in his own handwriting, revealing websites he visited, trips he took along with men he met and what they were going to wear, and other details.

My thought at that particular moment in time was, "Why you dirty dog!" I believe in Karma my friends. What goes around comes around, and he can no longer deny the truth nor do I care to hear his false words. All in all, years later, I have my proof and it is written by his hand.

PROFILE #35: SUE T., 48, California, dated two years, married 24 years, divorced three months, three children, financial sales management.

When Tom and I married in 1982, I believed that we were best friends and had a solid foundation for a marriage. We shared a faith in God, passion for developing a connected relationship with one another, and conviction about marriage and family. We met in college and started our friendship by sharing hopes, challenges, ideas and dreams. Humor and intellect were instant connectors for us; we thoroughly enjoyed one another's company.

The families we grew up in were similar - and yet, very different at the core. I am the oldest of four girls. Born in the Midwest, my family moved to the West when I was just six years old. I was raised in a Christian home and although fairly strict, I later came to appreciate being raised by "square parents." They introduced me to the security of faith-based living and fostered this by being active in an extended church family. Sexually, I lacked experience as I was raised to value being a virgin at the time of marriage.

Tom also grew up in a conservative Christian family and spent his childhood in the Midwest. He is the third of four boys and although he grew up in a loving home, his childhood was stressful as the family struggled to cope with a substance-abusing father. His mother did the best she could to raise the boys within that context and keep life as "normal" as possible. His sexual experience was also limited, and he professed to be a virgin as well at the time we married.

Post disclosure, Tom revealed that he remembered me asking him once (very soon after we met in college): "Are you gay?" When he told me this recently, I asked, "How did you answer when I asked?" He said, "No." I honestly do not recall even asking him this question and even though I was very aware of Tom's unique sensitivity, intuitive nature, artistic ability, musical inclination and interest in all sorts of various topics and people, it did not cross my mind that he might be gay. After all, he was interested in sex with me, and expressed himself with ease. From my perspective, we were very attracted to one another. Ours was a NATURAL and COMFORTABLE relationship from the moment we met. The fact that we were also best friends and trusted one another made this relationship stand out from others, and it just felt very "right" that we wanted to be married.

We met at a small Christian college in the West and grew close over the course of two years. I was a junior when he arrived on campus as a freshman. Our first meeting involved humor – we shared laughter instantly. We worked together on the college newspaper and as a result of this and numerous other activities, we learned that we had much in common and that our differences complimented one another.

Looking back, there were a number of "red flags" that I wished I would have acknowledged as they revealed themselves during our 26-year relationship.

Red Flag #1: Over-Analyzing (Justifying) the Relationship

We were the only couple I knew during the late 70's/early '80's who visited with a Sociology professor about personality and compatibility tests, went to a major university for assessments about career preferences, attended *Engaged Encounter* before marrying and sought out books and resources on how to cultivate the best relationship possible. Then, just before marrying, we counseled with a pastor (which was not as unique given our Christian upbringing). How many outside sources should it take to "justify" a relationship? At the time, this exploration felt right and served to affirm our relationship. Looking back, I wonder if we were trying to "make it work" given the disclosure of him being gay?

Red Flag #2: "Running Away" from His Family of Origin

Tom was intentional about coming to the West in order to "run away" from his family of origin, blaming them for his unhappiness and stifled creativity. He was desperate to be liberated from life with an alcoholic father who was unpredictable and often the cause of embarrassment and pain. He resented his two older brothers who taunted him about his art and invited him to feel shameful and inferior. He faulted his mother for not leaving her marriage and freeing the boys from the trauma of living with the effects of alcoholism. The only person he spoke fondly of was his younger brother, with whom he was often excluded from family interventions and other important decision-making. The two "little boys" were sheltered from crisis, and as a result, clung together to maneuver through rough times. Family discord was always present and Tom preferred to have as little contact as possible with his family throughout our marriage.

Red Flag #3: Secrets Lead to Shame and Tragedy

Tom's biological grandfather (on his father's side) committed suicide when Tom's father was just an infant. Then, Tom's own father (who was an alcoholic for most of Tom's upbringing) also committed suicide after Tom left for college. From what was pieced together about the suicides, the first appeared to stem from not being able to face the truth about selling fraudulent goods (the grandfather was accused of misrepresenting goods that he had sold) while the second may have been prompted by an inability to cope with learning the truth (his father had not been told the true story of his own father until very late in life). In short, these suicides – both on his biological father's side of the family – pointed to a history of secrecy, shame and tragedy. If history predicts the future, his could be riddled with uncertainty. Statistically, one of the four brothers might have a propensity to end their own life. At the time we married, these were the only red flags I saw about our relationship, but discounted them because I believe that love and the ability to face challenges honestly can conquer anything. As it stands now, I wonder if his family history fostered Tom's self-deception about his own sexual orientation. One thing was for certain---being faced with truth in this family had already resulted in tragedy at least twice.

Red Flag #4: Looking to Replace the Love of a Father

At the three-month marker of our marriage, Tom went to San Francisco to research a job possibility. While staying with a male friend (who had participated in our wedding and was openly gay), he called me at 2:00 a.m. one morning with a confession, "Sue, I just kissed him..." The story went something like this: He and this man had dinner, great conversation and after a few drinks, lay on the floor and shared a passionate kiss. Tom was terrified as he made the disclosure to me. As for the listening and digesting of the news, I was horrified and in shock. I did not know what to think although I recall ALWAYS wondering if there was more to the story. After all, I was thinking about the few times when I had been drinking and how kissing always led to wanting something more.

I told only one person; a cousin of this gay man's who was a trusted friend of both Tom and me in college. We weighed the possibilities and probably we both chose in some unspoken way to avoid the obvious: Two men kissing – one a declared homosexual and the other newly married – probably meant that there WAS a sexual meaning/reason. In a strange way, I think we both did not WANT to know that which we didn't know... if that makes any sense at all.

We were college-educated for Heaven's sake! Two men kissing should have been a VERY OBVIOUS RED FLAG. And yet, two college-educated women talked it through and came to accept it as understandable and forgivable given the circumstances. I told no one else about the kiss – not anyone. I was too ashamed, embarrassed and scared for what this might mean for our marriage.

173

When Tom returned home, we sought the counsel of a marriage and family therapist. Over the course of the next year and a half, it became evident that Tom had "missed the love of a father" and that the kiss was likely a way for him to fill a very real void. This was an answer that made perfect sense given his absent and alcoholic father who eventually chose to abandon the family by taking his own life.

I trusted Tom and never doubted his word. After all, he had instantly called me and confessed the kiss on the very night it occurred… there was nothing to hide and after many discussions with the expert counsel of a therapist, I trusted this final resolve to be the truth.

I knew that this kiss – in the context of being married - was an act of infidelity. However, it was, after all, JUST A KISS and it had gone no further. After the numerous therapy sessions and deep soul-searching that was required, wasn't it perfectly understandable that he longed for the love of a father?

Red Flag #5: The Seven-Year Wait to Have Children

Although we had decided to have children even before marrying, it took me seven years to finally forgive Tom for the kiss. It wasn't until that length of time had passed that I actually was able to finally let go of my doubt and trust that it was okay to have children. If I had been honest, courageous enough to TRUST my own intuition and self-confident enough to leave him (despite my religious convictions), I could have SAVED me and my three children from an immense amount of pain. I regret not being courageous enough to face up to what a passionate kiss between men could mean; it seems absolutely crazy to me now that I could not see it then. This seven year window of "wondering" should have been enough for me to acknowledge that something just wasn't right.

Red Flag #6: Hiding and Leaving

Tom has always been charming and quite a "people-person." It was wit and charm that probably first attracted me as he had a way about him that instantly warmed a group and got people talking. At first, his charismatic personality was unique and engaging. However, his big personality allowed the "real him" to hide behind an articulate, funny showman. He always had just the right surprising remark to make in any situation – his intellect, humor and vocabulary supported him well to deflect attention.

Over the years, I began to notice that a refined sarcasm had woven its way into Tom's way of being. His joking could be cutting and hurtful. He became critical of others and would complain about the actions or words of our friends after a social event. He increasingly felt the need to openly criticize others, and sometimes I judged this as being rude and unnecessary and was embarrassed by his "honesty." Pointing the fingers towards the faults or inadequacies of others must have somehow made him feel better. To this day, he points at the extra weight I carry to invite me to feel badly so that he can feel better about his choices and himself.

Towards the last few years of our marriage, it was not uncommon for Tom to actually disengage and remove himself from the ending of a dinner or night out. We would be at a friend's house for dinner sitting around the table, and all of a sudden, we'd notice that Tom had left the table and was watching TV with the kids, or reading a book he'd brought, or he was ready to leave. It was easier to schmooze, use sarcasm or even remove himself from an activity rather than face the discomfort of what was the truth: He was a homosexual "acting" in a heterosexual life.

Red Flag #7: Blaming Others

From the first time I met Tom, it was clear to me that he was a victim of his "terrible childhood". His father drank constantly and eventually committed suicide; his mother stayed with his father – enabling the drinking to continue; his older brothers chided him into self-doubt and his teachers gave him poor grades because he was "too creative." As adults, when we realized that our expenses outweighed our income and that we would need to make more money, he couldn't increase his income because he didn't have an advanced degree. Then, after spending $40,000 to get a Master's degree, he couldn't make more money because he decided that he didn't value money more than the happiness he felt in his current position. The focus on needing more money then became MY FAULT because then he turned it around to point out that I valued money more than happiness!

It didn't really matter WHAT happened; he was the victim and it was always someone else's fault. In the early phases of our relationship, I played "hand and glove" into this routine as I was the oldest child of four girls and readily took Tom under my wing to encourage him to be himself and pursue his artistic talents. In the end, it was everybody else's fault that he chose to hide his homosexuality and instead, marry and have three children. It was even MY FAULT that he chose to leave me after his disclosure as my anger was so intense that it "drove him away"! He has often said that he "would have left me even if he wasn't gay" because of my anger and hurt. This blaming followed a 24-year period of being best friends and lovers in a relationship that I valued and trusted as being real and genuine. Being a closeted gay and living a fraudulent married life for 24 years was not HIS fault; it was now MINE! It became easier to tell his family and friends that I was "too controlling, too angry and too mean" to stay with.

In The Aftermath

In writing this, at 10-months post-disclosure, I must admit, I feel like a fool for not having recognized the KISS for what it was: a desperate cry for help that screamed, "I am gay!" I feel so foolish for: 1) not having TOLD more people so that I could have gotten more input at the time and maybe made a better decision for my future, and 2) for not SEEING how truly obvious/overt this red flag was! True love, believing what Tom SAID (rather than what he had DONE) and my religious convictions about marriage, all won out at the time to blind me from seeing his real truth.

Although I would never trade my three beautiful children for anything, I am clear that I would NOT have married a man who I did not believe valued our love as much as I did. I believed in our sacred commitment and would have honored it. After all, if he truly is gay – then, he HAS BEEN GAY for all of this life... and so, WHY wouldn't I continue the marriage? I thought that it had been a good, honest and true marriage – one that many people spend a lifetime to find. So, WHY THEN does being gay give him a free pass to leave his marriage and break up the family he chose to create? I'll probably never understand how infidelity becomes "necessary" if a spouse comes out as "gay" – that somehow the gay spouse NEEDS and DESERVES a more complete sexual life. No one ever DIED from having a less than complete sex life! I also acknowledge that my blindness to this probably stems from my unending love for him – much as it did at the time of the man-to-man kiss.

I trust that my broken heart will eventually heal and that I will come to understand how this shattered reality became my life. I pray that I am on the path to forgiving myself first for blind ignorance – and then Tom for deceiving me and then, after disclosing his truth, for choosing a gay lifestyle over our marriage and family – so that we are able to lead the kids to a healthier place. My belief is that whatever love did exist between Tom and me will be strong enough to move us into a new relationship so that we can continue to raise the children with love and compassion. I also trust that God will ultimately reveal a good purpose in this painful journey. There is a great opportunity just waiting to unfold and I cling to this knowledge with a faith-filled hope and confidence.

Conclusion

The stories you have just read are all true stories. Nothing has been changed except some of the names. The way you can tell they are true is because it would impossible for 35 women from around the world to all come up with stories that had such different circumstances, but such similar feelings, emotions, and events.

After reading these stories, I hope it gives any woman who may be wondering if her husband is gay or not enough information to draw the conclusion she is seeking.

Allow me to summarize some of the lessons learned from this book:

1. No two gay husbands are exactly alike, but they all share some of the same characteristics.

2. Most women have sex lives that slide downhill quickly; however, there are a few that have sustained sex throughout the marriage. Don't let that fool you. As many a gay man says—he can "pretend" or "fantasize" about a man and still have successful sex with a woman.

3. Your husbands are living a lie. Most of them have become professional liars who can spin amazing stories and fairytales. Don't be naïve and believe their stories.

4. Nearly 50% of all men will NEVER CONFESS. You can spend your life being a detective, or you can just accept that you know the truth even if he won't admit it to you. If you're expecting a confession, you'll waste a lifetime trying to get it.

5. Straight men are not "gay curious." If a man is looking at gay porno, he's looking at it to become sexually aroused-- not to satisfy his curiosity.

6. Don't believe that gay men who live with women don't cheat on you while they are married. They do.

7. Don't believe that your husband doesn't have time to cheat. It only takes 30 seconds and it can be it the bathroom of a restaurant where you are dining.

8. Gay doesn't go away. You can't make it happen and you can't make it end. No matter how much you wish it away--it stays.

9. Beware of men who live their lives in denial. They can say "no" to you about being gay, but they are saying "yes" to a man—at least as far as sex is concerned.

10. These marriages don't get better. In fact, the longer you stay in them the more debilitated YOU become. Your self-esteem and sexual-esteem will be stripped away one layer at a time.

11. In many cases, the gay husband will blame you for the failure of the marriage. You were too pushy, too nagging, too demanding, not attractive enough, not understanding, and not supportive. Instead of arguing the fact, just accept it's because of their guilt and lack of ability to accept responsibility. Don't feel defensive—you are listening to the viewpoint of a man who doesn't understand rational reasoning.

12. Gay married men often go out of their way to isolate you from friends and family. This is their way of keeping "control" of you and the situation. If your marriage is not on happy, solid grounds, don't allow yourself to move somewhere far away and lose your support system.

13. **Having a bad relationship with a father does not cause a man to become gay.** That's a bunch of hogwash that some money making, unethical professionals are using to

give gay men false hope about becoming straight. It is also giving you false hope that your gay husband can change. The logic is insane. If that were the case, why isn't every woman who had a bad relationship with her mother a lesbian? How about gay men that had a good relationship with their father? Why are they gay?

14. Gay is genetic. **It is not a choice.** Being honest about it is where the choice comes in. You can't blame your husband for his homosexuality, but you can blame him for not being honest with you at the point he knew he was gay.

15. Some men take a long time before they can acknowledge that they are gay because they are trying so hard to be straight. They really aren't looking to fool you—they are looking to fool themselves.

16. If your husband/man tells you that he is Bisexual or likes Transsexuals, this means GAY. It doesn't matter what you call it or how you dress it up, it is what it is. Once a man wants a penis, it's gay. Call it whatever makes YOU feel better, but eventually you have to face it is GAY.

17. If your husband tells you he'll never do it again, don't fall for it. He may mean it at the moment he's saying it, but it won't last. It can't last. He's gay. He needs a man to satisfy him.

18. If you are still having sexual relations with your husband and you suspect he is gay, HAVE PROTECTED SEX. Too many of our women are suffering with sexually transmitted diseases. When in doubt—do!

19. Some gay husbands have sociopathic and/or narcissistic behavior. This is a very common trait. Sociopathic means they have a lack of conscience and find it easy to blame you for everything that is wrong in your marriage and in his life. This way he doesn't have to take responsibility for

anything. Narcissistic means that they are self-absorbed and self-centered.

20. No matter how much money you spend on yourself to make yourself beautiful, no matter how much weight you lose, no matter what plastic surgery you have—it won't change your gay husband. He won't want or desire you any more or love you any better. Don't waste your time and money.

21. Stop wasting time and money going to marriage counseling or therapists trying to make a broken marriage work. These marriages cannot be repaired. They are broken beyond mending. You can waste years looking for ways to fix it, but all you lose is valuable years of your life and throw money down the drain.

22. Many women tell me that they are staying in their marriage because of the children because they don't want to break up the family. Your children will know if you are unhappy and internally blame themselves for it. Don't fall back on the excuse that you are staying together for the sake of the children. Children often know before you know about their fathers, and then they feel the guilt of keeping it a secret from you because they don't want to hurt you. Do the right thing by your children—walk away from a marriage that doesn't exhibit love, kindness, passion, and compassion. Children repeat our mistakes—it's learned behavior. Walk away because you want your children to model themselves after your strength—not your weakness.

23. Gay Husband Recovery doesn't come in a day, a week, or a month. It may take a year or more. You will go through many stages during the recovery time from shock to denial to anger and keep repeating this cycle. Anger is fine as long as it doesn't become bitterness. Anger helps you because it means you are standing up for yourself. But if you don't get past the anger, it turns into bitterness—

WHICH ONLY HURTS YOU!!! We all recover eventually, but the time of recovery depends on your willingness to accept things for what they are and then move ahead. That being said, the anger may resurface every time there is an incident concerning the children or finances. It's okay. Get angry—you can even go and have a pity party. But you need to find support to move past it or you'll keep getting stuck.

24. Chances are, your husbands did love you when they married you. In some **rare cases**, they didn't as you can see from the stories. For the ones that did, they were hoping that their love for you would be strong enough to make them into someone who they are not. They can't. In time, it has to crumble and fall apart. And remember—as much as a gay man loves you, it can never be the kind of love that will truly fulfill you for a long period of time. He can never understand the love that a straight man can give you.

25. There are some excellent gay ex-husbands. I know this because I have met them. They try to help women and men who come to me by giving generous support. If all of our ex-husbands were this way, life would be much easier. I thank those men for "doing the right thing." They are kind to their families even if they aren't living in the same household. This is the best of all possible solutions. Unfortunately, it doesn't happen often enough. To my gay men who give this support, thank you so much for caring about others who are in pain.

26. Life does go on, and in many cases it goes on much better. Once you know the root of your problem, you can start to repair your life.

27. Stop blaming yourself for not knowing or not seeing the signs. When you love someone you always want to think the best of them. We don't understand homosexuality and

how it can come into a marriage. Homosexual means "same sex." Why would we think a gay man would marry us? Even if you had some inking before the marriage, you didn't understand that love wouldn't push it away. We were brought up in a generation that acknowledged "sexual experimentation." We thought even if someone did try it in his younger days, it was experimenting. It wasn't. It was gay. We learned the hard way.

28. Learn to trust your judgment because this is the best way to move ahead. It is normal to feel that every man is gay when your marriage ends. This is not the case, but we lose our perspective. It does come back later on.

29. Some gay men have multiple marriages. Just because a man is older and should have come to terms with himself doesn't mean he does. About 20% of my women have gay ex-husbands who marry again. They feel very hurt. They shouldn't—they should feel hurt for the unlucky woman who now has to deal with the lies and deceit again.

30. There are some horrible straight men out there. If you jump too fast to find a man after your marriage ends, you will most likely meet up with one of them. Take the time to get to know yourself again as you were before the marriage. Take time to rebuild your life and figure out how not to make the same mistakes. Work on building up your self-esteem and sexual-esteem which has been stolen away from you.

31. The husbands in these stories have come up with typical gay husband excuses for anything that seems odd to you. LEARN TO TRUST YOUR INSTINCTS. If it feels wrong—it is wrong. Stop trying to make excuses for the inevitable.

32. The quickest way to start to heal is to find support. I am available to any woman who needs support through my books, free monthly newsletters, pain pals for one-on-one

support, and my online support chats conducted three times a week. All you have to do is write to me at **Bonkaye@aol.com**, and I will get you all the support you need to keep moving "straight" ahead.

About the Author

Bonnie Kaye, M. Ed., author of *How I Made My Husband Gay: Myths About Straight Wives*, is internationally recognized as a counseling expert in the field of straight/gay marriages. Since earning her Master's Degree in Counseling in 1986 from Antioch University, she has counseled over 30,000 women who discovered their husbands are gay as well as 2,000 gay men who needed support in coming out to their wives.

Kaye started her counseling after the demise of her own painful marriage to a gay man in 1982. Her first book *Is He Straight? A Checklist for Women Who Wonder*, first published in 2000, has helped thousands of women understand the dynamics of marriage to a gay man. She has three other books on this subject: *Doomed Grooms: Gay Husbands of Straight Wives* (2003); *Man Readers: A Woman's Guide to Dysfunctional Men* (2005); and *Straight Wives: Shattered Lives* (2006).

She has appeared on international, national, and local television and radio to explain how this phenomenon happens and the damage it does to a marriage. She is a consultant for the major television talk shows including *Oprah, Dr. Phil, Montel Williams,* and *Tyra Banks*. She has appeared on national shows including *Oprah*, *CNN with Paula Zahn*, and *FOX News*. She has also been interviewed by numerous publications as an expert in this field including *Soap Opera Digest* and *Cosmopolitan Magazine*.

Kaye's two websites, which can be viewed at **www.Gayhusbands.com** and **www.Straightwives.com,** have ranked number one on the Internet search sites since their inception. They offer information including how to subscribe to her free monthly newsletter "Straight Talk," which has a readership of over 7,000 people internationally. Kaye also conducts an online support group three times a week to lend support to women during and after their marriages.

In addition to counseling, Kaye is a director in a non-profit post-secondary adult school in Philadelphia, developing and implementing education and job skills training programs. She also owns a GED Center in Philadelphia which prepares adult students for the high school equivalency exam.

LaVergne, TN USA
01 April 2011

222630LV00002B/22/A